RENOVATED

A Wife According to God's Design

THE BIBLE STUDY

By

SUSIE WALTHER

Renovated: A Wife According to God's Design

©2025 Susie Walther

P.O. Box 272
Odessa, FL 33556
thewelltraining.org

Written by Susie Walther
Edited by Tarah Todd

ISBN: 979-8-9912197-5-4

Published by The Ghost Publishing, LLC

To my husband Bob,
my greatest cheerleader, who has faithfully championed
and encouraged the work of God in my life. Through
you, God has done so much in me. I am, and always
will be, forever yours.

To the countless, amazing women,
married and unmarried, who have taught me, and
graciously allowed me the privilege of teaching them.
I am a better woman because of you.

To my Lord and Savior Jesus Christ,
Who did not have to choose me or use me, yet He
did. My life belongs to Him who loves me and has
transformed me for His glory and my good.

Forget the former things; do not dwell on the past.
See, I am doing a new thing! Now it springs up!
Do you not perceive it? I am making a way in
the wilderness and streams in the wasteland.

Isaiah 43:18-19

Table of Contents

A Word from the Editor

I walked into The Well women's Bible study in the fall of 2010. I didn't know that all my paradigms were about to be upended, but they were. Like a desert traveler, discipleship was like water to my weary soul. I didn't know how thirsty I had been.

Much to my dismay, my husband's career moved our family to Houston, Texas, in 2017. There were many things I didn't want to leave in Florida, but I couldn't believe God planned to separate me from The Well when it had made such an impact on my faith. A couple of years went by, and I slowly drifted from my convictions about discipleship.

One silver lining that came out of the pandemic was that The Well started online Bible studies. As I sat on Zoom with women from all over the country refreshing my memory on all things discipleship, I again felt like a desert traveler finding fresh water for a second time! Also because our worlds were on Zoom, I began teaching Writing and English Grammar online to my homeschooling friends. The mom of one of my students is on staff at The Well. When Susie lamented at a staff meeting that she needed an editor, I came to mind. The rest is history.

While I've been editing The Well's conference content for five years now, this is by far our most extensive project. I've attended *Renovated* several times and I've seen the positive impact it has had on me as a wife and on my marriage. I've hosted the livestream *Renovated* at my church in Texas, so I've seen with fresh eyes how this content can bring clarity to some of the struggles we face in marriage. I've edited the binder material for *Renovated* and seen how the content grows and changes as Susie and I learn more and engage in discipleship with married women with each passing year.

As we entered into this book project, I had some misgivings. It seems so permanent to print something in a book without the safety net of knowing you have the freedom to tweak it in a couple of years. My faith is constantly growing and changing. I don't believe everything I believed five years ago. Jesus loves us too much to let us stay the same, and I am thankful for that, but my journey has made me skeptical. What if I don't agree with this content five years from now?

My other hesitation stems from the reality that everyone does not agree with everything they hear at *Renovated*. Sometimes our lack of familiarity with one another can lead to misunderstandings. Sometimes we have differences in our deeply held theological beliefs. But if you disagree with something you hear at the conference, you have the opportunity to talk to your small group leader or the friend that brought you. There are women at the conference who have known Susie and can attest to her heart for you and your marriage. ALL of that is lost for a stranger reading this book, disconnected from the discipleship culture of The Well. How can we say some of these very difficult things in a cold, printed book? What if you're reading this alone with no one to help you process it?

As I wrestled through my misgivings, I'm thankful that Jesus met me in the struggle. In marriage and in everything, we follow our powerful risen Lord, not words in a book. This content doesn't have to be "perfect" because Jesus is already perfect on our behalf. I trust that the Holy Spirit is guiding this process, from the first day Susie shared these concepts around her kitchen table, to the day you read those same concepts in this book. Please read this in community and work these principles out together. God loves you and He loves your husband. My prayer is that He will use this book to help you grow closer to Him and surrender your marriage to Him.

As I bring this word from the editor to a close, I want to express my gratitude. I thank Jesus for orchestrating events so that I could help with this project. I praise Him for how He brought Susie and me together and how our strengths and weaknesses complement one another. I would also like to thank Susie for trusting me enough to let me be a collaborator in addition to an editor and for patiently and gracefully dealing with my grumpy reactions to some of her grammatically awkward passages. I would like to thank my husband, Thom, for loving me faithfully before I became a *Renovated* wife. I have not always been fun to be married to, which makes me appreciate his loyal, steadfast, Christlike love all the more. I also want to thank Thom and my kids for how supportive they are of my work with Susie. She and I often spend hours hashing out prepositions and subordinate clauses, not to mention theological premises. My family is very patient with my extended absences or random survey questions about their grammatical preferences. If you find an error in this book, I want to know!

Tarah Todd

A Word from Susie
– An Introduction

I love being a woman!

I've said that many, many times. However, recently, someone asked me why I love being a woman. I had to think about it because stating *how* you feel is much easier than explaining *why* you feel the way you do. I thought it would take a while to drum up an answer, but it spilled out of my mouth before I thought of how it might insult the person who asked.

"Because I see my husband, and I'm so happy I'm not him."

It was a man who asked the question, but he grinned and took it graciously. Honestly, I don't even know all the reasons why I'm glad I'm a woman and not a man. I just know, deep down inside, that I like being female.

Now, don't get me wrong. Just because I'm glad that I'm not my husband, doesn't mean I don't love my husband! I adore him. He's my perfect-for-me-imperfect man, as I'm his perfect-for-him-imperfect woman. At the time of this writing, we've been married for 34 years, and I look forward to the "still counting" part!

Even though I love being a woman, I recognize that there are major challenges for women in our culture, in the church, and in marriage. If we're keeping it real, our capacity for nurture, compassion, and kindness as women is often confused with weakness. Our contribution can be overlooked and undervalued. What makes us different from men can be perceived as a disadvantage, and the list goes on.

I've experienced those challenges on top of personal and family challenges. I'm bi-racial, I have a quadriplegic sister, my parents divorced when I was young, I was molested by a close cousin, I was raised in two different cultures. I don't need to go on. I'm sure you get it.

Then there are spiritual challenges we face as women if our God-given gifts and callings have no place to operate in our churches. This reality can often create frustration, apathy, and even resentment, but the greater loss is when a woman loses confidence that her personhood and contribution matter to the Body of Christ.

Yet I still love being a woman, and I love the ministry I have specifically to women. I have a passion for helping women see their worth and value in the eyes of God, even if others don't, and more importantly, even if the women themselves don't. I love helping women rise above lies they have always believed, go further than the limitations others have put on them, and start living out their purpose right where they are.

My ministry is to women from every race, age, and denomination. It's to single women, brides-to-be, current wives, ex-wives, and widows. I minister to rich ones, poor ones, shy ones, loud ones, and even the ones with attitude. And of course that ministry includes women with kids, women without kids, empty nesters, and everyone in between.

I can share so many stories of victory with you, but that would make for a VERY long introduction. Suffice it to say that I've witnessed women with a history of affairs (committed by them or against them) forgiven and set free. I've seen hopeless, passionless women revived. I've watched women wrecked by addictions (theirs or someone else's addiction) walk in victory. I've seen marriages on the brink of divorce restored. I know women who were once disempowered yet now walk in purpose and with confidence.

Irrespective of my own failures and imperfections, God has given me the privilege to be a part of many women's stories, even if it's been just a small part. And I can say this, if you read this book and do the work, you'll be the *next* woman whose life is changed for the better, in Jesus's name.

The foundation of my ministry to others is the Bible. However, I know that teaching and advice derived from a biblical worldview is not always culturally sensitive or politically correct. How can it be when the world's passions, and so often our *own* passions, have fallen so far away from God? But the unpleasant truth about truth is that it's not meant to make us feel good. It's meant to transform, inspire, and strengthen us, making us agents of change from within.

The ministry I lead is called The Well Training Ministry, Inc. It is a training and discipleship ministry for women. One of our conferences is called *Renovated: A Wife According to God's Design*. I have led this conference for over a decade, and the results and testimonies have been humbling. It's not just the way God has touched the many women who have attended. It's also the joy I've experienced serving alongside so many devoted women *and* men who have rolled up their sleeves so we can create a space where God can bring revelation, renewal, and restoration to so many.

However, I've been sharing the material in this book for more than 30 years, well before it grew into a conference, because the *Renovated* journey started with me! God used this content to save me from myself as a wife, and to save my marriage. So, I have three decades of memories and have witnessed transformative shifts in the lives of countless women, shifts that have often led to healed and renewed marriages, just like my own.

Much of this material is anecdotal and keeps evolving! It's the result of crying out to God for years, studying Scripture, and reading books. I have listened to lots of other women and observed the fruit of their ideas and choices. I have chosen to seek out good counsel. And most importantly,

I just keep applying what I learn, no matter how painful it is, to my own life and marriage.

As you read what's on these pages, some things may sound familiar to you. Like you, I've internalized much of what I've read and studied over the years and now it's all mixed in. If I knew who to give credit to, I would! Regardless, I want to pass on to you what I've gained from others, from my time in the Word of God, and from my own experiences.

I continue to yield my perspective and adopt God's perspective as the blueprint for marriage. As I do this, sometimes kicking and screaming, I can honestly say that I've experienced personal transformation, and my husband benefits from it!

I pray that this book finds you *before* you need it or *when* you need it. I pray that you are not only ready to read it, but ready to do the work so that *you* can be set free, empowered, and uplifted as a woman, wife, or bride-to-be.

I pray that this book will have an immediate impact on your life, that you would sense conviction, a need to repent, a renewed hope, a fresh awareness, the humility and courage to change for the better, and a desire for God's will over your own.

I pray that this book will strengthen your marriage (or future marriage). I also pray that your marriage won't follow the pattern of the world, but that it will be revitalized, more peaceful, and more unified. I pray that God's Kingdom culture would inform your family decisions, so that there is a deeper level of understanding, compassion, and consideration toward one another.

I pray that this book will have an impact beyond just you as an individual. My hope is that once you have experienced the freedom from this journey, that you would take the initiative and lead *other* women through this book in your homes, workplaces, schools, churches, or neighborhoods. We need to be in the fight for the family, one wife at a time.

But I pray that this book has an even greater impact on the discipleship of others. As you engage in a small group with other women, my hope is that discipling relationships would emerge and blossom with more and more women mentoring one another. *(Shameless plug – attend our women's conference, Operation Train Up a Woman: Breaking the Cycle of Non-Discipleship!)*

But know this – one of my prayers has already been answered simply because you're holding this book right now! It might not have every answer for all the brokenness you or your marriage face, but I truly believe it holds *an* answer that can be the beginning of your hope and healing.

They say that you "find what you're looking for." If that's true, then be on the lookout for God to speak as you delve into this study. God's Word to you may come from the Scripture you read, a prayer prayed in your presence, something said in the course of a conversation, or as you prepare for your group meeting. It doesn't matter *how* God speaks to you. The promise stands – *God will speak!*

So, listen. Look. Think. Meditate on the Word. Make every effort to apply at least one truth from this book to your life and marriage because truth sets us free. Do the work, and I promise you – God will meet you where you are. It doesn't matter if your husband changes or not, or if your marriage changes or not. *You* will change.

Welcome to *Renovated*, my sweet sister.

Susie Walther

Leading a Renovated Group

This Bible Study is ONLY for those who:

Have *never* done a Bible study before
Have done a Bible study before
Have done *many* Bible studies before

Welcome to a new and exciting 9-week journey! It is a meaningful journey – not a sprint, not a Netflix binge, not a shortcut to happiness, and not something to be dismissed. This is a sacred, intimate, nitty-gritty conversation between you, God, and a few brave women.

This study is designed for small groups, where the content will have its *maximum* impact. You can study this book alone, however discussing the content with a trusted friend will *increase* its impact.

How to start a group:

Begin praying. Pray for God to "show" you women you could invite – whether they're women you know or just met.

Put a group start date on your calendar. We do what we schedule ourselves to do, NOT what we intend to do! So, schedule a date, and then keep praying.

Start inviting. Invite women from work, church, women sitting in the bleachers with you, through your social, etc. And if someone tells you that they'll come to your group, ask her to invite a friend. The *size* of your group doesn't matter. The woman or women who show up do.

Don't talk yourself out of it. Starting a group will be intimidating if you focus on yourself and all the things you *can't* do. Just focus on Jesus and all the things He can do *through* your YES!

Before you meet:

Set aside time. That means phone-on-silent, coffee-in-hand, and if you have kids, then kids-bribed-with-goodies kind of time. Oh, and about that phone, God shouldn't have to compete with Instagram and Facebook Reels. Give HIM your focus and He'll reward you with clarity.

Don't wait until the last minute. Don't just skim through the pages. Do the work. No great thing ever results from just doing the bare minimum. Look up the Scripture verses, think through the content, and apply what stands out to you in each chapter. That's how a breakthrough happens.

How to maximize your small group time:

Keep it safe. Your group members (including you!) need to guard what they hear, which is how we guard each other's dignity. Gossip and judgment *destroy* trust. Protecting vulnerability *builds* trust.

Be honest. Be bold enough to say, "I'm struggling," or "That hit me hard," or even, "I don't get it." Being honest opens the door to new conversations that will lead to revelation, and even healing. *Tip: keep a box of good tissues on the table.*

Have an open mind and a receptive spirit. It's okay, normal even, to not like or agree with everything you read. However, growth rarely comes from staying in your comfort zone or only reading what confirms what you *already* believe. Stay open. Stay humble. Let God speak – even if it's not what you expected.

Share your takeaways. Don't just read. Connect. Share. Your voice matters. Your story matters. Your perspective might be precisely what someone else needs to hear. First, we need to hear God speak *to* us, then we need to allow God to speak *through* us.

Have food on hand. Snacks at a Bible study are always optional, but it makes deep, theological, keep-it-real conversations a little more relaxed and enjoyable.

Create common ground. At your first meeting, include a SHORT icebreaker. Talk about how your time together will flow and set up a snack list. Praying and eating together and sharing takeaways every week will help the group relate to one another.

Pray. That's your secret weapon – the doorway to clarity, peace, and power. Every step of this journey, pray to recognize the voice of the Holy Spirit. Pray individually, as you prepare each week. Pray as a group each time you meet. You'll be amazed at what happens when you pray in your "closet" and when two or more pray together.

Get our free resources. There are resources in English and Spanish on the Well Training Ministry website, including: Snack Sign-up Template, 8 Steps to Develop a Habit in God's Word, How to Memorize Scripture, Who I Am in Christ, Enemy Knowledge, Sexual Betrayal, and more. *thewelltraining.org/free-resources*

Scripture memory:

You'll find that most every chapter has a memory verse because Scripture memory is an important spiritual discipline and spiritual asset. It can help us fight sin and temptation from within and without by increasing our awareness of God's truth, thereby influencing our choices.

The memory verse in each chapter is in the New International Version (NIV) unless otherwise noted. However, feel free to choose another translation. There are lots of apps and strategies for memorizing Scripture. Ultimately, you need to find the tool or way that works best for you. The following is one tried and true method:

Day 1: *Write it out.* Jot down on an index card:

> The reference (e.g., Mark 1:1)
>
> Topic (these are pretty much already done for you – Perspective, Helpmate, Submission, Sex)
>
> The whole verse
>
> The reference again

Follow this pattern for memorizing: say the reference, the topic, the verse, and the reference again. Read it out loud several times for 30-60 seconds.

Day 2: *Break it up.* Divide your verses into phrases. Repeat the reference, topic, and the first phrase of the verse several times. Say this out loud for about 30-60 seconds.

Day 3: *Add to it.* Memorize another phrase from the verse, always starting with the reference, then the topic/title, etc. Say this out loud for 30-60 seconds.

Day 4+: *Wrap it up*. After you can correctly recite what you've learned, add more phrases from the verse. Continue until you've memorized the whole verse. Don't forget to say the reference at the end!

During your group time, share your memory verse. It's not about saying the verse perfectly. Remember, it's about hiding God's Word in our hearts to help us make more godly choices!

Sample meeting agenda:

15 mins   Arrival

> Have coffee/tea/cold drinks available; have a snack sign-up, let everyone get settled

25 mins   Prayer

> Have everyone share one prayer request and one praise; depending on the size of the group, divide into twos and threes and pray for each other's request and praise

10 mins   Scripture Memory

> Most chapters include a suggested Bible verse to memorize; have each woman who memorized the verse recite it to the group

15 mins   Accountability

> Have everyone share their practical application of what they learned and implemented from the previous chapter; celebrate and encourage each other

45 mins   Content-Directed Discussion

Section by section, have everyone share what stood out to them in the chapter and their answers for *some* of the questions

10 mins   Wrap-Up

Remind them who signed up to bring snacks next time, share any last thoughts/comments, ask someone to close the group in prayer

Seek the help you need:

This book is just that, a book. It is not a substitute for professional counseling or advice. Some of you are in a critical state relationally or personally, and you need qualified help.

If you are in an abusive relationship, you need to get out, get safe, and pursue the information and services you need to stay safe and stop the abuse.

If you have had an abortion, you would greatly benefit from being in a post-abortive recovery group.

If you have experienced sexual betrayal, you are experiencing trauma. You need a professional counselor who can help you process and heal.

If you have experienced traumatic events that have not been resolved, you need counseling and/or pastoral care so that the past doesn't continue to negatively impact you and your relationships.

If you or someone you love struggles with addiction, you need to find a recovery group for support and accountability.

Bottom line: get the help you need to be whole and free. Don't delay for any reason. Life is too short, and life is MORE than what you're living right now.

A Renovated Prayer

**Dear Heavenly Father, You are the King of the
universe and Lord of our lives.**
We come before You with hearts surrendered
and eyes fixed on Jesus, the Author and Perfecter
of our faith. You are the fountain of all wisdom,
and we acknowledge that apart from You,
we can do nothing.

Let Your Holy Spirit be the Counselor, Teacher, and
Guide to each woman participating in this Bible study.
May every woman be filled with the knowledge of
Your will in all spiritual wisdom and understanding.

You are the God who makes a way in the wilderness
and rivers in the desert, so we trust You to bring
every detail of our lives and relationships
into alignment with Your good and perfect
will, even those details and circumstances
that seem impossible to us.

Father, we boldly pray that every participant in
this study will be enlightened and transformed

by Your Spirit. We ask that women would be
inspired, equipped, and empowered to lead
others through this study, reminding them that
they already have Your permission and authority
to help others grow spiritually. May this study
join the ripple effect that we have already seen
through *Renovated*, which has brought
new life to marriages and families.

Use this study, Lord, to draw women who never
expected to teach into the joy of leading,
and to help women who have felt unseen
discover their voice through its pages. Let it be
a tool of true renewal, not only in knowledge,
but in our hearts, relationships, and in our
identity as followers of Christ.

Lord, let *Renovated* be more than a title –
let it be an overwhelming testimony and a story
of how You rebuild what was broken, restore
what was lost, and renew what has grown weary.

We dedicate this book to You, Lord, along with
every seed it will plant and the fruit it will bear
for Your glory alone.
In the mighty name of Jesus, Amen.

Renovated

The Bible Study

CHAPTER 1

Setting the Table

What All Women Want

If you're reading this, then this is what I know – you're a woman. I also know that you're either married, or would like to be married, or know someone who's married.

As women, we *all* have something in common. Deep down, we want to be *chosen*, adored, cared for, respected, appreciated, and most importantly, we want to *feel* loved. Really. Feel. Loved. That includes wanting to be protected and provided for, and not just monetarily. We want safety for our emotions and help with our fears, and we *don't* want to be cared for purely out of obligation. We want to have the type of relationship where we are fully seen and still highly valued regardless of pimples and cellulite, hair loss and wrinkles.

We want to be free from the experience of betrayal. We want both interdependence and independence. We want to feel so safe that we can spread our wings, be ourselves, share our thoughts and ideas, and never lose our ability to laugh.

Many of us grew up dreaming of our Prince Charming. For some he's Mr. Tall, Dark, and Handsome. For others, he's a Blonde, Blue-eyed Ken

Doll. But Prince Charming can also be that Quirky, Funny, Tech Guy who can make you laugh until you cry (and you know what can happen when some of us laugh like that!). But *all* of us want that strong, yet tender man who gives us a listening ear, says the right words at the right time, and is a consistent-but-not-annoying presence.

In general, we long for perfect – the perfect man, perfect relationship, perfect children, perfect cheekbones, and the perfect body without dieting or having to work out. We seriously long for perfection.

The problem is, we dream of a fairy tale world when, in reality, we live in a fallen, dysfunctional, fractured world. So, there really is no such thing as the shining knight on a mighty steed who will *always* choose, adore, care for us, and never hurt us. But they do hurt us, which leads many married women to one main conclusion: *I know I'm not perfect, but I'm pretty sure my husband is the problem.*

I get it because I've been there. But this book in your hand is *not* a husband's Bible study. It's a wife's Bible study. So, we're not going to play the blame game. That stinks, I know. But real change starts from within, so we just need to make the effort to take an honest look at ourselves in the mirror.

Doing that is necessary because despite how jacked up your husband (or future husband) is with all of his issues, we also bring our own junk into the marriage. Stuff like:

Unresolved woundedness and unaddressed traumas

Unhealthy coping mechanisms: addictions, escapism, control, codependency, etc.

Identity issues and/or negative self-image

Coveting what we *think* others have (e.g., thinking that *her* knight is still on his horse, while ours fell off a long time ago!)

2

Hoping the marriage or our spouse will fix what's broken in us

The effects of a pornified, hyper-sexualized culture

Fear of failure as a wife or mother

Childish ways of communicating

Unforgiveness or bitterness

A spirit of competition or resistance to cooperation

A tendency to put family, children, work, and every other thing before our husband

A negative attitude toward authority and submission

A need to *fix* or *save* our husband instead of letting the Holy Spirit do His work

Pride: believing you're better than your husband

Self-righteousness: believing you're less of a sinner than your husband

Lack of a vibrant, intimate relationship with God cultivated by intentional, committed fellowship and followship of Jesus (which would positively impact all the above listed junk!)

That's the short list! So, even though it's easy to focus on our husband's junk, we need to find the mental and emotional bandwidth to focus on our own junk instead.

Look up *Matthew 7:3-5*. Write out this passage in your own words.

_____

_____

_____

_____

_____

What is a "log in your eye" that you are aware of right now?

_____

_____

_____

_____

_____

My marriage was on the brink of destruction

I know that many of the things on that list are true for you because they were true for me. I became disillusioned with the man who definitely was *not* my shining knight and determined that he was the *whole* problem. A very strong emotion became my reality - I HATED BEING MARRIED. Though there were some marital perks, my pain and frustration easily overshadowed them to the point of despair and deep regret for saying "I do."

After another day of fighting, in which neither of us listened to each other, I left our apartment in tears. It was raining so hard, and I was crying so hard, that I had to pull over. The ugly cry turned to yelling and banging on the steering wheel. I remember yelling to God, "Why did You let me marry him?" (Because, you know, we always blame God for our freewill choices.) "He's SOOOOOOOO immature! Why did You let me marry him?" The struggle was real.

Then, it felt like God joined me in the car and was sitting in the passenger seat. In my spirit, I heard God calmly answer me, "To help him."

What? I waited for more... but that was all there was. *To help him.*

Help him? I didn't want to help my husband. He was a grown man for crying out loud. But that phrase completely arrested me. Our argument didn't matter anymore. God had my attention. *"To help him,"* I whispered.

The problem was, I had no idea what that meant! What in the world would that look like in real life? In *this* marriage?

I didn't know anything about a good marriage. My parents divorced when I was entering middle school. I didn't know anything good about sex; I was molested by a cousin. My father married the woman he had an affair with while married to my mother. When it came to defining family, all I knew was brokenness.

Well, the rain stopped, and I came back to the apartment. I walked past my husband without a word and sat on the floor by our bed. He came into the bedroom slowly, almost like he was making sure the coast was clear. He sat down next to me and didn't say a word, which was fine because I wasn't ready to say anything either.

Eventually, I spoke up and said very flatly, "God created us to be supported by a five-cord strand: emotional, spiritual, mental, social, and physical. Emotionally, well, you're an Army Special Operations guy, so I don't think you even know what an emotion is. That makes it hard to talk through or resolve anything with you. Spiritually, you're barely crawling when it comes to your faith, so I have to get my spiritual needs met elsewhere. Mentally, you don't care about anything outside of cars and the Army, so I have to find good conversation apart from you. You only want to hang out with me and sleep, so we have no social life."

And then I said, "That leaves only the physical, which amounts to me doing the two things you can buy, and I will NOT allow myself to be reduced to a maid and a prostitute."

My husband had been divorced before. I knew deep down that he didn't want to be divorced again. With all sincerity, he said, "I don't know what to do or how to fix us."

And that's when I heard it come out of my mouth, "Then let me help us," to which my husband said, "Okay."

That was a life-changing moment for us. The only problem was that I *still* had no idea what "help" meant to God! And so a quest began.

How it all started

I found every instance of the word "help" in the Bible and saw a myriad of ways it was understood. I looked up the word "submit," since I knew it was part of the wife package. That was an eye opener. I gradually stopped defining submission based on how I *felt* about it or the way the world defined it. Honestly, I was pretty blown up over the difference! Then I looked up how the Bible talked about sex, since you know, God was the one Who created it, and He created it to be experienced *only* within marriage.

After months of asking God questions, searching for the answers, praying, reading, meditating, and listening for God to speak, my head and heart exploded. Then my head and heart started to change. I also began applying this Word-inspired knowledge in my marriage. And then it started happening. *Our marriage was being Renovated.*

One day I shared my findings and testimony with a friend in my accountability group. She said, "Susie, you need to share this with other women."

And so it began. It took courage but I started sharing my big marital ah-has in living rooms and small groups. I saw the effect it had on women, even though I didn't have any of them in mind when I began this journey. I was purely in my own marital survival mode. Isn't that just like God to turn His work in you into His work *through* you for others?

In 2011, inspired by a friend's vision, we brought these lessons to life as a conference. Each time we host the conference, women leave with binders full of material and they share it. And God keeps doing it! What He did in me and through me, He's doing in and through them, and using this material to equip women and strengthen marriages.

But we saw the need for the content to be in a more accessible format for those who hadn't experienced the full conference. So, here we are. We created what you are now holding, *Renovated, the Bible Study.*

You're going to feel some things when you do this study

As you read this book, you may feel some things you didn't expect to feel. I want you to know – it's okay. God loves you and He wants you to conform to His image. God wants to help you live His dream for your life and marriage. That means He's going to make it personal, and the Holy Spirit is going to let you see things in yourself or your marriage that need to change.

When God shows you something, you have a choice to make:

Defend against the truth and decide to remain the same

Respond to the truth and decide to change

I want to encourage you from now – please don't get stuck and don't shut down! Commit to processing whatever discomfort you may feel as you read, because there really is something good waiting on the other side of that emotion.

Some of you may need to push through denial because generally speaking, when it comes to problems in our marriages, we rarely see ourselves as contributors to the problem. We tend to believe very strongly that we aren't the ones who need fixing. But truth be told, every human being needs fixing in one way or another!

You might need to push through some anger because I'm probably going to say something that'll make you want to throw this book across the room. But I need you to know – I'm not *trying* to offend you or tick you off. *But* I'm also not going to pull any punches or play any word games trying to say what I need to say without actually saying it.

7

Some of you may need to push through feelings of guilt as you realize your marriage isn't what it could be because of choices *you've* made. You have to keep from being paralyzed by that feeling, especially since Jesus stands ready to forgive and renew. It's not complicated, and renewal is knocking at your door. Here's one of my favorite verses that leads us to the experience of God's forgiveness:

"Repent, then, and turn to God, so that your sins may be wiped out, and times of refreshing may come from the LORD." Acts 3:19

Some of you might feel discouraged because your marriage is already in a deep hole and the way out seems insurmountable. God's Word offers you hope:

"Forget the former things; do not dwell on the past. See, I am doing a new thing! Now it springs up! Do you not perceive it? I am making a way in the wilderness and streams in the wasteland." Isaiah 43:18-19

What is the "new thing" you see God doing in the midst of your wasteland?

_____

_____

_____

_____

_____

A Promise

Contained in this book is the power to reshape your life, and possibly even your marriage, but you have to do the work. If you make the effort to apply at least one truth to your life and marriage, that truth has the power to set you free. I promise you that God *will* meet you where you are – in your anger, in your depression, in your confusion and frustration, in your shame, in your loneliness, in your lies, in your jealousy, in your pride, in your lust, and in your worldliness. He'll meet you behind your make-up, under your job title, and in your heart.

We also added a unique surprise: little secrets that can help you better understand the man you married. Throughout the book you will "see" into the mind of a man in what we call, *A Man's Perspective* by our publisher, Eli Gonzalez. Naturally, no one guy can speak for his entire sex. However, I promise you that hearing a man's vantage point can help you learn what you don't generally know because you're a woman…not a man.

Now let me remind you again, YOU are taking this study, not your husband. It doesn't matter if your husband changes, the promise I make to you is *not* for him; it's for you. The important thing is to let God do a new thing *in* you because that new thing *changes* you. Jesus wants to help *you*, whether your husband or marriage changes – or not. So, girl – RUN after that promise!

CHAPTER 2

Gaining a New Perspective on Marriage

Your Perspective Determines Your Experience

Perspective matters because it determines your attitude, emotions, and experience, just to name a few. However, when all is said and done, *your* perspective is just *your* point of view. It may be "your truth," but *your truth* may not be *the* truth.

Your perspective is also *subjective*. For example, did the rain bless the farmer or ruin the picnic? Your perspective on the rain is driven by your expectation or desired outcome.

Your perspective impacts your ideas about marriage and your role in it. Whether you're married or single, what is "your truth" about marriage? What is your expectation of the marital experience or desired outcome?

_____

_____

_____

_____

_____

Now, let's consider the word "renovate." It can be defined as:

To repair to a previous better condition

To restore to life

To revive or rebuild

Your perspective on something's *value* determines whether or not you're willing to renovate it when it needs repair. You wouldn't renovate something you didn't consider good or valuable. Marriage and your role as a wife are valuable. If you're honest, your perspective on both could benefit from some renovation to experience the type of marriage God designed and desires you to have.

Now, if you're single, you need to remember that this is a marriage study. It's not a study on singleness. However, you're still in the right place. I would even dare to say that you're in a better place because you have the opportunity to start a marriage without baggage, bad routines, emotional triggers, or bad memories that are hard to forgive. This study can help you understand God's perspective on marriage and allow His truth to define your attitude, role, and contribution within a marital relationship. So, if you're single, you won't have an answer for all of the questions in this book. Just answer what you can and don't worry about the rest.

Let's recap:

> Your perspective determines your experience (and a lot of other things too!).
>
> Your perspective isn't *the* truth, it's just your point of view.
>
> Your perspective is subjective and deeply connected to your expectations.
>
> You will only renovate something if it's valuable in your perspective.
>
> You're in the right place, with the right book, and this is the right time, whether you're married or single.

What is *your* reason for choosing to do this study?

_____

_____

_____

_____

_____

Your Worldview Shapes Your Perspective

Whether you know it or not, or can admit it or not, the bottom line is – you've been indoctrinated. You are not a clean slate. All of us are conditioned by culture: social culture, family culture, religious culture... you name it. Most of you reading this are also influenced by 21st century Western culture, which is essentially anti-Bible and post-Christian. Post-Christian basically means we've been flavored by Christianity, while rejecting its claims and implications.

Since we've been conditioned by Western culture, we are also extremely individualistic and rights-oriented, and that preset impacts the way we interpret and apply information about men, women, and marriage. Add to

13

that all the "isms" in our culture: sexism, feminism, denominationalism, racism, materialism, nationalism, humanism, etc. These "isms" are in the very air we breathe. They govern the way we live our lives, and our ideas of right and wrong, good and bad...without us even knowing it.

The content for *Renovated* is rooted in a Christian worldview predicated on the Bible. So, before we can legitimately have a marriage discussion, we must have a worldview discussion because your worldview impacts your perspective. *And your perspective determines your experience!* Because *Renovated* is rooted in a Christian worldview, just about *everything* you read here is going to be counter-cultural.

Now, there isn't just one kind of Christian worldview. But the good news is that every Christian worldview, irrespective of our denomination or religious experience, has in common the Bible as its foundation. Ultimately, the Bible is about God and His Kingdom. The Kingdom of God is about the rule of God in and through our lives. This impacts our relationship with God, others, and ourselves as individuals. *Matthew 22:36-40*

The Kingdom of God is counter-cultural and counter-intuitive to us. That means it's the opposite of our way of thinking, being, doing, and relating to each other. God's Kingdom is supernatural, and His ways have to be learned because they are *not* natural to us.

Every worldview has key assumptions, and a couple key assumptions within a Christian worldview are:

The Bible is a revelation about God. It's NOT a book about us. It's a book about God *for* us.

The Bible is authoritative. God is the only authority over it. It claims to be the Word of God to us. Time doesn't diminish or negate its truth, which means its message is still relevant today.

Your worldview matters to your perspective, and at some point, your perspective will clash with the biblical perspective. When that happens ask yourself:

Do I believe the Bible is a God-made book or a man-made book? Answering that question determines your honest response to what the Bible says.

If you believe God is the authority behind the Bible, you will *not* dismiss it when you don't agree with it. Whether you accept the Bible by faith, by reason, or both, you will accept what it says because God is the authority behind the Book.

If you *don't* believe God is the authority behind the Bible, then you will disregard what it says and default to your own worldview. It's just that simple.

What is the benefit of aligning your thinking with the Bible?

Psalm 19:7-11

_____

_____

_____

_____

_____

John 8:32

_____

_____

_____

_____

_____

Romans 12:2

_____

_____

_____

_____

_____

What is the danger of clinging to our own ideas?

Proverbs 12:15

_____

_____

_____

_____

_____

Proverbs 14:12

_____

_____

_____

_____

_____

Romans 8:5-8

_____

_____

_____

_____

_____

If the Christian faith is new to you, or you're unsure about what it means to be a Christian, or you would like to have a relationship with God, but don't know where to start, I invite to you read *Why a Relationship with God Matters – and How to Begin* on page 145 of this book.

Let's recap:

You are not a clean slate.

The Christian worldview is based on the Bible.

The Bible is about God *and* the Kingdom of God.

The Bible is authoritative.

When you and the Bible disagree, be ready to realign your thinking.

Seven Renovated Perspectives

Since *your perspective determines your experience*, gaining a new perspective has the potential of leading to a new experience. Some of these perspectives may be new to you. Let's explore!

1. You are either building or destroying your marriage.

Proverbs 14:1

"The wise woman builds her house, but with her own hands, the foolish one tears hers down."

Building or tearing down. Those are the only two options. To put this into context, this wisdom, or lack thereof, has nothing to do with your intelligence, education level, career successes or failures, etc. You can have an eighth-grade education and be the wise woman and you can have a PhD and be the foolish woman. So, don't assume anything about yourself, and just be honest as you go through this exercise.

Discovery questions to see if you're BUILDING your house:

Do you pray for your husband regularly? *I'm not talking about that whispered prayer we've all prayed, "Lord, please help me not injure this man permanently!"*

    Yes ___ I could do better ___ No ___

Do you use manners when talking to your husband? *You know, little things like: Please. Thank you. Good morning. You're welcome. Excuse me. I'm sorry. Would you mind if…*

    Yes ___ I could do better ___ No ___

Do you exercise self-control by not saying everything you *feel* like saying or acting on everything you *feel* like doing? *Making the same self-regulating choices you'd make with a friend, stranger, or someone you respect?*

    Yes ___ I could do better ___ No ___

Are you physically affectionate? *Do you let your husband hug you randomly and do you randomly hug him? Do you initiate holding hands or sitting next to him on the couch, text a kind word to him, tell him you're grateful for him?*

    Yes ___ I could do better ___ No ___

Discovery questions to see if you're TEARING DOWN your house:

Does your husband hear criticism from you daily? Regularly?

    Yes ___ I could do better ___ No ___

Do you try to make him feel like an idiot or incompetent because he doesn't think like you?

    Yes ___ I could do better ___ No ___

Do you compare him to other men, to his face, in your head, or with your friends?

Yes ___ I could do better ___ No ___

Do you blame him for most, if not all, of the problems in your marriage?

Yes ___ I could do better ___ No ___

Dear sister, you have tremendous power to positively or negatively impact, not just your husband, but everyone in your home. The choice to be wise or foolish is up to you.

What will you do THIS WEEK to begin building?

_____

_____

_____

_____

_____

What will you do THIS WEEK to stop tearing down?

_____

_____

_____

_____

_____

2. The authority over your marriage matters.

Your marriage is being influenced by the one leading it. Your marriage can be under God's authority, OR it can be under your own authority. What it *can't* be is under God's authority AND *your* authority at the same time!

Paraphrase *Matthew 6:24* in your own words:

_____

_____

_____

_____

_____

You choose the authority over your marriage, and the authority *you choose* determines the kind of fruit your marriage produces. There are a lot of people who call themselves Christians who are married to other people who call themselves Christians, but their marriages are not under God's authority. As a result, their marriages aren't producing the fruit God designed a marriage to produce. *(And I'm not talking about having kids!)*

The Bible gives us clarity on what God's fruit looks like in our lives and relationships. Look up *Romans 14:17* and *James 3:13-17* and write down what would characterize a marriage under God's authority:

_____

_____

_____

_____

_____

Is your home characterized by peace (not necessarily quiet) or chaos? Is there patience or short-temperedness? Respectful discussion or yelling? Helpful compromise or crying to get one's own way? Is there *any* fun or laughter in the home?

I know, you may be thinking: *Whoa, wait! There's no such thing as a perfect marriage or a perfect wife.* Yep. That's true, but we're not talking about *perfection.* We're talking about a life, marriage, home *governed* by peace, mercy, and all those good things. Living under God's authority doesn't mean you'll never have fights, or problems, or bad moods, etc.

That's not the point *and it's not even the question*. The question is – who is leading your home, God or you? And you know the answer by what characterizes your home. So, I'm talking about the consistent fruit, not the temporary flare-ups. As the years go by, marriages led by God will increasingly bear better fruit.

Who or what has been leading your marriage? *Examples: parents (yours or his), addictions, culture, the lifestyles of your friends, your emotions, your kids and their schedules, the tyranny of the urgent, etc.*

_____

_____

_____

_____

_____

What is ONE aspect of God's fruit you would like to experience in your marriage?

_____

_____

_____

_____

_____

What do you need to do or stop doing to begin experiencing that fruit?

_____

_____

_____

_____

_____

3. Your marriage is part of your discipleship.

I'm not sure any of us enter marriage thinking about our discipleship. We don't walk down the aisle eager for the challenges in marriage that God will use to conform us to His image! Discipleship can be defined in many ways, but ultimately discipleship is about transformation. It's God's mechanism for removing the ugly that is in us and replacing it with an aspect of His nature. And God will use anything to make you like Christ, including your marriage.

What do these verses reveal about what God wants to work out in you:

Romans 8:29

_____

_____

_____

_____

_____

2 Corinthians 3:18

_____

_____

_____

_____

_____

Marriage helps us see who we really are. *Just so you know,* who you are at home is who you really are. That's the plain truth! The privacy of our homes becomes God's laboratory to strip off the pleasantries and niceties we fake when we're in public. We can see where the evil hides in our hearts and makes its way out through our mouths and actions.

Before you can confront a sin, you must identify it. Then you have a choice to make. Change and adopt the habits of Heaven or stay the same and continue in the habits of hell.

In what ways has God used your marriage to uncover what's hidden in you? *Examples: self-righteousness, feeling sorry for yourself, greed, lying, lack of self-control, etc.*

_____

_____

_____

_____

_____

4. Your marriage is like a baby.

We all know about the birds and the bees – and that babies are born from a *physical union* between a man and a woman. The baby is its own being that needs to be cared for and nurtured to survive. Your marriage is like that baby! A marriage is "born" from the *spiritual union* of a man and a woman when they say their, "I do's." Much like a newborn baby, the marriage needs to be nurtured and cared for to survive.

Let's imagine a scenario where the man doesn't want to take care of your young baby. I doubt you would say, "Fine! Then I'm NOT going to take care of the baby, either! It can stay in its poopy diaper and scream its head off. AND if you're not going to feed it, then I'm not going to feed it either. So, our baby can just go ahead and starve to death!"

No one would do that to a baby unless they're a horrible parent! You would take care of that *baby for the sake of the baby*, regardless of the other person's choices because *you* helped bring that child into the world.

Well, the same thing is true with your marriage. SOMEONE NEEDS TO TAKE CARE OF THE MARRIAGE FOR THE SAKE OF THE

MARRIAGE! And just because your husband won't take care of it, doesn't eliminate your responsibility because *you* helped bring that marriage into the world! So, beware of refusing to do your part because your husband isn't doing his. Now, the "baby" might still die, hear me clear on that – but at least you know you did what you could to keep it alive.

Is there anything you're refusing to do in your marriage because of what your husband is refusing to do? What's one thing you can do to take care of your marriage for the sake of your marriage?

_____

_____

_____

_____

_____

5. Your husband might feel hoodwinked by you.

According to the dictionary, to be hoodwinked is to be deceived or tricked by someone.

So, here's the deal: If you and your husband were unbelievers when you got married and then you committed your life to Jesus *after* the fact, you need to know that he didn't see that coming! And now, you're probably NOT the same woman that he married.

That's a tough one for men, because they marry us hoping we *never* change. We marry them, hoping that they *will*!

But your husband didn't ask the Christian version of you to marry him. He popped the question to his favorite party girl or the version of you that made him feel like he was a king. You said "I do" to the sinner he was, and probably still is! Now, you're trying to get closer to God, but he's thinking *this isn't what I signed up for!*

Your husband's perspective determines his experience. He's not thinking about how good it is for your soul that you're growing closer to God. He may be asking, "Where's the woman who dressed the way I liked, talked the way I talked, watched the movies I watched, and who went to the clubs, bars, parties, and walked on the wild side with me?"

But what are you supposed to do? Walk away from Jesus for your husband? No, girl! Instead, you must help your husband *like* this Christian version of you! You have to help him see how much better it is to be married to Christian you. But, HELLO, religious you isn't going to win him over. Self-righteous you, and holier-than-thou you isn't going to win him over either.

Your husband has to experience something *good* and beneficial from you – a new level of kindness, trustworthiness, some respect, some encouragement, some affection, some forgiveness. Something! Anything!

If *you* find a new way to treat him, not only might he fall in love with the new you, but he might also want to know the God who changed you and brought stability and peace into his home.

And I know some of you are like, "Susie. Girl. *I'm* the one who got hoodwinked! I thought my husband was my knight in shining armor. I thought he only had eyes for me. I believed him when he said for better or worse, for richer or poorer, in sickness and in health. But he's not the man *I* thought *I* married!"

I hear you and my heart hurts with yours if you're that wife with a broken dream of a husband. Your anger and disappointment are justified. However, without realizing it, you can make the leap from being disappointed in him to punishing him. But you're broken dream isn't going to be restored by punishing him. That road leads to more pain and the destruction of your marriage. Know this, dear sister: your marriage

25

may be in disarray, but God's plan is not for you to suffer or stay broken because of your husband's sins, lies, or failures.

So, take your pain to God. That's not cliché or meaningless Christian jargon. That's a strategy for healing. Let God comfort and repair your heart through prayer and His Word. Get good counsel to help you process your feelings and learn how to talk to your husband in constructive and instructive ways that can lead you both to something better. You aren't *the* key to change, but you're certainly part of it, even if the only change is in you.

How have you changed since you said, "I do?" *Examples: spiritually, emotionally, physically, mentally, socially, etc.*

_____

_____

_____

_____

_____

Would your husband say that change has been for better? Why or why not?

_____

_____

_____

_____

_____

6. Marriage can't save us from sin.

Seriously, only Jesus can do that. Look up *Acts 4:12* and paraphrase it in your own words:

_____

_____

_____

_____

_____

A sin cannot be cured or redeemed by marriage. However, the enemy tries to convince us otherwise. A guy can think his porn addiction will go away when he gets married, but marriage can't fix a porn addiction. A woman might think her problem with money will go away when she gets married, but marriage can't fix greed. Marriage can't fix addictions, unprocessed trauma, mental health issues, lust, pathological lying, lack of self-worth, not feeling pretty enough, or anything else for that matter.

Marriage is good in God's eyes. It's a holy union that brings blessings, and God can use it to grow us and refine us – both individually and together. *But it just can't save us from our past or from ourselves.* And...if you need your marriage to fix something in you, you'll wind up making your marriage an idol. Only Jesus can fix you.

What did you think marriage would fix in you or for you?

_____

_____

_____

_____

_____

7. Every wife needs to calibrate.

No matter how long you've been married or how great your marriage is, every wife needs calibration. Why? Because God designed a wife's role with two essential elements: Helpmate and submission.

None of us are perfectly calibrated as wives and we can't stay calibrated without intentionality. Some of us are naturally inclined towards being a Helpmate. Others of us are naturally inclined towards submission. That means we must intentionally cultivate the component that is *less* natural to us.

The illustration below highlights what calibration and miscalibration of Helpmate and submission produce:

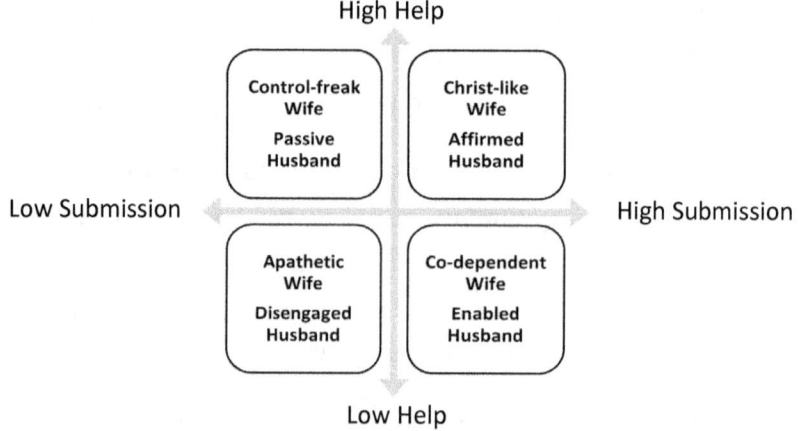

If you calibrate towards High Help and High Submission (top right), you will grow in your Christian faith and as a human being, and your husband will feel loved, confident, and affirmed.

If you are miscalibrated towards High Help and Low Submission (top left), you will morph into a controlling/manipulating woman and will wind up with a husband who capitulates and quits being pro-active in the relationship.

If you are miscalibrated towards Low Help and Low Submission (bottom left), you will both be unhappy, unmotivated, depressed, and probably divorced-minded.

If you are miscalibrated towards Low Help and High Submission (bottom right), you will most likely be co-dependent and will wind up creating a monster because you tolerate what you shouldn't tolerate.

We will never be perfectly calibrated because we are humans. However, we must always be intentional to seek calibration, or we will just keep slipping away from God's design for wives.

Where would you plot yourself on the illustration?

_____

_____

_____

_____

_____

What is the fruit of your current calibration or miscalibration?

_____

_____

_____

_____

_____

What is your next step toward calibration? *(Remember, it will feel unnatural!)*

_____

_____

_____

_____

_____

A Man's Perspective by Eli

→ A husband can tell whether or not his wife believes in their marriage. Your words and actions tell us "You matter, we matter, this covenant matters" or that you're biding your time until you can find a way out. Either way, you will get fruit from whatever seed you sow. Most husbands really do want to fight for their marriages, but we need to know that you are fighting for the marriage, too.

→ Many men get married hoping it will cure our weaknesses, but it doesn't. We need Jesus for that. What we really need, is for you to encourage us to do better without trying to fix us. Reward even minor improvements, e.g., made healthy choices, didn't yell today, helped around the house, decided to stay home with you and not hang out with the guys, watched a chick-flick with you (even though you fell asleep). Just show him more appreciation than rebuke.

→ Don't hold your "holiness" over our heads. A husband knows when his wife thinks she's better than he is. If someone thinks they're not good at something, they won't want to do it. So, if you constantly say things like, "I can't believe you always...," "I would never do that...," "The Bible says that a man should...," then he won't want to try. Maybe the reason he won't go to church with you is because you'll make him feel like a hypocrite? Remember that you're a sinner, too, and he's dealing with your weaknesses just like you're dealing with his!

Which "Man's Perspective" caught your attention and why?

_____

_____

_____

_____

_____

Words of Declaration

Let these statements become part of your prayer this week. Saying them out loud individually and/or with your group can be powerful. With Jesus's help:

I will value my marriage as worth renovating.

I will align my perspective on marriage with God's design.

I will be a builder of my home, not a destroyer.

I will do my part to put my marriage under God's authority.

I will cooperate with the Holy Spirit as He uses my marriage to transform and conform me.

I will care for my marriage for the sake of the marriage.

I will give my husband something to like about the Christian version of me.

I will let Jesus alone fix me.

I will continually calibrate Helpmate and submission.

In Jesus's name. Amen.

CHAPTER 3

The Helpmate:
Our Purpose in Marriage
Part 1

Scripture Memory Verse
*"Since the creation of the world, God's invisible
qualities – His eternal power and His divine
nature – have been clearly seen and understood from
what has been made, so that we are without excuse."*
Romans 1:20

Gaining a Biblical Perspective

One of the biggest questions we have for ourselves is: "Why am I here?" We ask it in a few different ways, "What's my purpose in life?" "What's my destiny?" People search the moon, the stars, their ancestors, horoscopes, fortune tellers, and everything else to find the meaning of life. I'd like to suggest that the answers are not found in *any* of those things. They are found only in the Bible because God is the Creator of Heaven and Earth, and He created people *on* purpose and *with* purpose. I encourage you to investigate the Bible's narrative for the answers to those deep questions.

Women are asking big questions, too, and looking for even more specific answers. "Why did God create women?" "What's my purpose as a single woman?" "What's my purpose as a married woman?" The good news is the Bible also has the answers to those questions! Let's start with a foundational verse:

Genesis 2:18

"The Lord God said, 'It is not good for the man to be alone. I will make a helper suitable for him.'"

This little verse is key to answering our questions and it also obliterates a lot of misinformation fed to us by this fallen world, and even sometimes by the church. Something we can't miss in Genesis 2:18 is that we were *created*. Sorry Darwin. God said – *"I will make..." That is a definitive creation statement.* You are not a biological accident. You are a deliberate, anatomical, psychological, relational, and spiritual design – made by God – to *be* a woman. Hallelujah!

The other thing we can't miss from Genesis 2:18 is that God said, *"I will make a helper...." That is a definitive purpose statement.* You are hardwired by God to contribute meaningfully to the lives of others. Your life *matters*.

But let's keep reading because God said something else that's pretty amazing! *"I will make a helper suitable for him."* You are an image of God (Genesis 1:26), created by God, to bring help to another image of God – your husband! Say what??? Eve was first created to help Adam. Then she had kids and helped everyone else, too!

The Apostle Paul understood Genesis 2:18 as a foundational creation statement. Look up *1 Corinthians 11:8-9* and write it out verbatim:

_____

_____

_____

_____

_____

The last thing we can't miss from Genesis 2:18 is this: *"The Lord God said, 'It is not good for the man to be alone...'" That is a definitive need statement.* Men were created with a *need* for our help! This does not mean that a man is "less than" or deficient without a woman. It means that the "good" God wanted Adam to do was not doable if Adam was alone. As a matter of fact, the only thing that was *not* good in all of God's creation was for Adam to be alone! So, yes, *God created Eve for Adam, but He also created Adam with a need for Eve.* That's a mind-blowing truth that balances the scales between a husband and wife!

So, here's what we need to understand from the get-go as women. We were *not* created by God to submit. We were created by God to help! Don't get me wrong. Submission has its place in God's relational plan, but submission is *not* why women were *created*.

What encourages you or surprises you about Genesis 2:18?

_____

_____

_____

_____

_____

Help Defined

Now we need to define the word "help" biblically, or we risk interpreting it through our tainted experiences, denominational lenses, and cultural ideas, etc. All of these corrupt and diminish the biblical meaning of the word "help."

The word for help in Genesis 2:18 is the Hebrew word *Ezer* (pronounced Eight-Zair). It means to: *surround, protect, assist, aid, and relieve.* I find it so interesting that the biblical definitions of Ezer fall into two categories:

Warrior qualities	Women surround and protect
Partner qualities	Women aid, assist, and bring relief

The biblical definition of help does *not* imply being a servant or a slave. It also doesn't imply being a controller, manipulator, or trying to take the place of the Holy Spirit!

BUT wait, there's more! God calls *Himself* an Ezer sixteen times in the Bible! The following verses are a snapshot of what is descriptive of God's help. Look them up and see what you discover.

Deuteronomy 33:26, 29

_____

_____

_____

_____

_____

Psalm 72:12

_____
_____
_____
_____
_____

John 14:26, 16:13

_____
_____
_____
_____
_____

Romans 8:26

_____
_____
_____
_____
_____

God created women in His image. One aspect of God's nature is that *He* is an *Ezer*. God created women after this part of Himself, making us *Ezers!* That means we have the BEST teacher ever on how to be a Helpmate because God is our blueprint. He is our model for what an Ezer is, what an Ezer does, and how to function as an Ezer!

You know what else that means? It means being the Helpmate in life or in marriage is NOT a lesser position or lesser role. You know why? Because God is not in a lesser position or lesser role as our help! He is still God, even as our Help.

The role of "Help" is an important and honorable role, and we see that over and over again in the biblical narrative:

Eve helped Adam

God helped Israel

The Levites helped the High Priest

Jesus helps the Father

The Spirit helps Jesus

The Church (aka, the Bride of Christ!) helps advance the Kingdom of Jesus on the earth

Christians are commanded to help each other

The angels help Christians

Do you get the point that the Helper is *important?*

How does this understanding of "Help" impact your perspective on your role and purpose?

_____

_____

_____

_____

_____

Write down a time when you experienced God as *your* Helper.

_____

_____

_____

_____

_____

Key Operating Principles for the Helpmate

There are at least two operating principles that undergird the biblical concept of Help. When we operate within these principles, we thrive and the people we're called to help thrive. When we operate outside of these principles, nobody thrives. Let's explore!

First Operating Principle: God's Authority and Law

The Bible declares that God created everything: men, women, children, marriage, relationships, animals, food, rain, the planet we live on, and the universe around it. God didn't consult us when He created *everything*. His designs are *His* ideas, under His authority, governed by His laws, not ours. *God's laws allow all created things to flourish and exist in harmony with other created things – if the laws are not violated or ignored.*

God created the laws that govern math, science, and all of nature. He created the laws of cause and effect, motion, gravity, energy, relativity, and everything else. We may not *like* all of God's laws, but we suffer consequences when we violate them. Why? Because they operate under *His* authority, not ours! For example, you don't have to like the law of gravity but violate it, and it might be the last thing you do.

God's laws also govern our relationships. The commands in the Bible teach us how to love God, love others, and love ourselves the way God intended. Very importantly, these relational laws teach us what love is and isn't, and what love does and doesn't do. *God's laws allow our relationships to flourish and for us to exist in harmony with other people – if the laws are not violated or ignored.*

So many of us struggle and are frustrated in our marriages and other relationships because we're *not* operating from God's relational laws.

Read the following verses and write out the relational commands in each passage:

Exodus 20:17

_____

_____

_____

_____

_____

Matthew 22:36-40

_____

_____

_____

_____

_____

John 13:34-35

_____

_____

_____

_____

The dot we need to connect is that the role of the Helpmate is governed by God's relational laws. _God's laws allow our marital relationships to flourish and for us to exist in harmony with our husbands – if the laws are not violated or ignored._

Second Operating Principle: God's Nature

The Bible declares that God has made His existence and character clear to us. Yes, God is Mystery, but there is also much about Him that is in plain sight!

Romans 1:20

"Since the creation of the world, God's invisible qualities – His eternal power and divine nature, have been clearly seen and understood from what has been made, so that we are without excuse."

There's a lot in that little verse that we're not going to touch. However, the thing I *do* want us to catch is that God isn't hiding Himself from us. He *wants* us to see Him, learn about Him, and relationally experience Him. So, though God is transcendent and beyond the limits of our five senses, He's made a way for us to see Him through what He has made. And this is the cool part: the *only* thing in all creation that God made similar to Himself, in His own image, is man and woman.

That means every man and woman individually bears the image God in his or her own right. However, key relational aspects of God's nature are revealed through the dynamic of the husband/wife relationship. *Ephesians 5:25-33*

Unfortunately, God's divine nature is no longer automatically revealed in men, women, and marriages. Both the image of God in men and women, *and* the husband/wife relationship have been adversely affected by the Fall of Man. *Genesis 3*

To course correct, we need to study the God of Heaven in order to know how to reflect Him on earth. That means *God* must become our blueprint for understanding maleness and femaleness, and He *must* become our blueprint for understanding how to relate to each other as husband and wife. Every time we stray from God as our blueprint, we mirror

41

something other than God. We end up mirroring the fallen world's views of men, women, and marriage, continuing to operate under the damaging influence of the Fall in our human nature.

In order for our marriages to reflect God's divine nature, we must recognize the qualities that are characteristic of Him:

God is One.

In Genesis 1:1, it says, "In the beginning God..." The word for "God" in the Hebrew is *Elohim* (pronounced El-oh-heem). The word is in the masculine *plural* form. So, in the very first sentence of the Bible, God's revelation of Himself is plural.

However, the Bible also reveals that this plural God is only *one* God. He is of one substance, yet exists in three distinct Persons, a Trinity or Tri-unity.

Read Luke *3:21-22*. How does each Person in the Trinity appear? What are They doing?

_____

_____

_____

_____

_____

If there was an equation for understanding the Father, Son, and Holy Spirit it would be 1 x 1 x 1 = 1 God, not 1 + 1 + 1 = 3 separate Gods.

If there was a marital equation for a husband and wife who are reflecting God it would be 1 x 1 = 1 flesh, *not* 1 + 1 = 2 separate people. *Matthew 19:6*

Bottom line: God is our blueprint for how two distinct individuals can be an integrated, harmonious "we" in marriage.

Additional verses on the Trinity:
Matthew 28:18-20; John 15:26-27, 17:20-21;
2 Corinthians 13:14; 1 Peter 1:2

God is communal.

The Father, Son, and Holy Spirit are in community with each other. Holy, selfless love fuels all their interactions. They don't just coexist. They actually participate in relationship with each other. Their participation involves having all things in common with each other, caring for one another, and clear communication.

Bottom line: God is our blueprint for how to be in true fellowship with each other.

Additional verses on the relationship between Father,
Son, and Holy Spirit:
Luke 10:21-22;
John 3:34-35, 17:22-26

God's nature is both masculine and feminine.

God's revelation of Himself is masculine, but the Bible also reveals that He made men *and* women *in His image.* The Bible uses language and metaphors that are both masculine and feminine to help us understand the male/female duality of God's nature. He's both Father *and* the God who birthed us.

One aspect of God's nature is not more like Him than the other, nor less equal or less valuable. God doesn't favor one facet of His nature over another. One part of Him is never jealous or envious of the other. He exists undivided and in perfect balance with Himself. He's not a sexist or a feminist. He's just God.

Men tend to reflect the masculine attributes of God because God made them according to the masculine aspect of His nature. Women tend to reflect the feminine attributes of God because God made us according to the feminine aspect of His nature. However, it is our masculinity and femininity *together* that reveal the fullest picture of who God is and He designed marriage to display this aspect of Himself beautifully. If one side is missing, we have an inaccurate picture of God.

Bottom line: God is our blueprint for displaying His nature in harmony as husband and wife.

Additional verses on the nature of God:
Genesis 1:27; Deuteronomy 32:18

God is interdependent.

The Father, Son, and Holy Spirit are not characterized by independence or co-dependence. There's no individualism or powerplays. They're not competing, controlling, or making decisions without each other. They function as a team.

The Father, Son, and Holy Spirit *choose* to cooperate with each other, which is beneficial, not detrimental, to their relationship.

Bottom line: God is our blueprint for how to work together as a team.

Additional verses on the interdependence of God:
John 5:30, 14:10; Luke 22:42

God submits to God.

The Father, Son, and Holy Spirit have *personal* equality, but they don't operate from *positional* equality.

Jesus said over and over again that He did nothing from His *own* authority. Jesus *has* authority, but He chooses *not* to exercise His authority over the Father. The Spirit *has* authority, but He chooses *not* to exercise it over the Son.

44

Bottom line: God is our blueprint for how to defer to one another.

Additional verses on the submission of God:
1 Corinthians 11:3, 15: 23-28; Philippians 2:5-7

God honors God.

The Father, Son, and Holy Spirit spend all their time honoring each other! The Father wants to glorify the Son. The Son wants to glorify the Father. The Spirit wants to glorify Jesus. The Father, Son, and Holy Spirit want all creation to see the greatness of each other! *Psalm 150*

Bottom line: God is our blueprint for how to honor each other.

Additional verses on the honor of God:
John 14:13, 16:14, 17:1, 4; 2 Peter 1:17

We have the blueprint for a happy, loving, healthy, flourishing marriage. It's God Himself! However, both husband and wife must strive to be the way God is. Either our marriages will reflect God, or they'll reflect the broken, fallen world around us. And we will always know what we're reflecting by the fruit that characterizes our marriages.

Which aspect of God's blueprint do you see expressed in your marriage?

_____

_____

_____

_____

_____

Which aspect of God's blueprint is missing in your marriage?

_____

_____

_____

_____

_____

Let's recap:

Women were created *on* purpose and *with* purpose.

God is our *Ezer* and He created women to be an *Ezer*.

There are relational laws that govern our role as the help.

God designed marriage (masculinity and femininity together) to *fully* reflect His divine nature.

God is the blueprint for a thriving Christian marriage.

Our Intrinsic Power

When God created women to help, He created us with an intrinsic power of influence because *you can't help who you can't influence.*

I'm not saying that you need influence to help someone sweep the floor or wash the dishes. I'm talking about the influence needed to impact someone's choices, perspective, and personal growth.

When we place our help under God's authority, and operate within His laws, we wind up using our influence to advance God's purposes. However, Satan is always tempting us to misuse our influence, which started with Eve in the Garden of Eden.

God created Adam and gave him the job of taking care of the garden. Satan had access to that garden, but there's no record in the Bible of him ever interacting with Adam.

Then God created Eve.

That's when Satan decided to have his first conversation with a human. He knew he had a play with Eve in the mix. A serpent or animal alone wouldn't be enough to sway Adam's allegiance away from God. However, another image-bearer, endowed with the life of God and created to help him, could possibly persuade him to disobey.

Satan preyed on Eve's *desire*. She took the bait and used her *influence* to get Adam to do something *she* wanted. The result: Adam chose Eve's offering of fruit over God's will for him, *and* them.

That kind of corrupted influence didn't end with Eve. We see women throughout the biblical narrative using their influence to advance their own will, focused on their own desires:

Sarah's desire to bring about the promise of God through her own idea caused her to influence Abraham to sleep with Hagar, which resulted in lots of dysfunction in her family. *Genesis 16*

Delilah's desire for money caused her to influence Samson to divulge a secret, which resulted in his imprisonment and eventual suicide. *Judges 16*

Zeresh's desire for her husband's happiness caused her to influence him to plot his rival's execution, which eventually resulted in her husband's execution. *Esther 5-7*

Jezebel's desire for power caused her to influence Ahab to worship her idols, and he wound up being one of the worst kings in Israel's history. *1 Kings 16-21*

Herodias's desire for revenge caused her to influence her own daughter to dance before a bunch of drunken men, so she could have the head of John the Baptist on a platter. *Matthew 14*

Don't think for a minute that Satan's strategy has changed! He still tempts us, *and he's tempting you,* to use *your* God-given influence in self-serving ways.

God has given us great responsibility as the Helpmate, which comes with great intrinsic power. We must learn how to wield that power for good. (FYI - that's the topic of our next chapter!)

Take an honest inventory of your influence.

When have you used your influence in a self-serving way?

_____

_____

_____

_____

_____

When have you used your influence to advance God's will for your husband?

_____

_____

_____

_____

_____

A Man's Perspective by Eli

→ Your husband didn't marry you because he wanted a helpmate. He didn't know he needed one. He married you because he thought you were the missing piece to his happiness.

→ Your husband is growing and changing just like you. So, stay curious about him. As his helpmate, ask him questions and continue to get to know him. Over the years, his different answers to the same questions may surprise you. Also help him find answers to the questions he's asking about you and about life.

→ Help refine his leadership. When he lacks vision, bring clarity. When he gets tired, depressed, or feels defeated, bring him strength through words of affirmation, back rubs, kissing his forehead, and remind him of the man you married. He doesn't need you to carry his load, but he does want you to make it lighter, even if he won't ask. The world forces us to be "MEN" outside the home, so let us recharge at home from time to time.

→ When it comes to your influence, your husband will take your advice often. However, your advice is not a mandate. He'll be more receptive to your advice if you are graceful (i.e. don't get grumpy or angry) when he chooses not to do things your way.

Which "Man's Perspective" caught your attention and why?

_____

_____

_____

_____

_____

Words of Declaration

Let these statements become part of your prayer this week. Saying them out loud individually and/or with your group can be powerful. With Jesus's help:

I will rejoice that God created me on purpose to be a woman *with* purpose.

I will do my part to reflect the relational aspects of God's nature in my marriage.

I will learn from my *Ezer* (the Lord God) how to be an *Ezer* to my husband.

I will learn to use my intrinsic power of influence wisely.

In Jesus's name. Amen.

CHAPTER 4

The Helpmate: Our Purpose in Marriage Part 2

Scripture Memory Verse
"A wife of noble character is her husband's crown,
but a disgraceful wife is like decay in his bones."
Proverbs: 12:4

Understanding Our Purpose

Now that we know that God created women to help, the big question becomes: What does God want a woman's help to accomplish? And very importantly, what does help even look like in real, everyday life? If help is our divine purpose, then we need to be crystal clear on what God means by "help." Let's explore!

God designed our help to function in three distinct ways: as the Helpmate, as a Mom, and as a Co-laborer.

1. The Helpmate: A Partner with God in your Husband's Purpose

In the first book of the Bible, not only do we learn *why* God created women, but we also learn *why* God created men:

To *obey* God	*Genesis 2:16-17*
To *work*	*Genesis 2:15*
To *love* a woman	*Genesis 2:18; 23-25*

Good gravy, that's nothing shy of glorious! What Christian woman wouldn't give anything to be married to a man who loved God, went to work every day, and loved her the way God wants him to love her???

When God created Eve to help Adam, it wasn't just to make him a sandwich. It was to help him be *great* by helping him *fulfill* God's purpose for his life! Um, you need to read that again!

Nothing has changed, ladies! To obey God, to work, and to love a woman is *still* your husband's God-ordained purpose, and God wants *you* to help your husband succeed in those three areas. Whoa, what?

It gets better. God actually hardwired your husband in such a way that he *needs your help to succeed* in what God created him to do! He can't become *that* great man without your help!

But hear me clear: your help is not for you to recreate your husband after *your* design. It's to partner with God as He recreates your husband after *His* design. But God isn't finished! He begins the work of re-creating *you* as you join Him in the process!

A husband benefits (and so does a wife!) when his wife fulfills her God-ordained purpose. How does the Bible describe that benefit to her husband?

Proverbs 18:22

_____

_____

_____

_____

_____

Proverbs 31:10-12

_____

_____

_____

_____

In light of what God created your husband to do, you need to evaluate your help. Ask yourself:

How can I help my husband obey God?

Well, for starters, God has already told us how to do this. We don't need to quiz our friends or come up with our own strategy. God Himself has laid out a 2-step plan for how a wife can help her husband grow in his allegiance to God:

Let's read *1 Peter 3:1-2*, and don't skip a word of it.

"Wives, in the same way, submit yourselves to your husbands, so that if any of them do not believe the Word, they may be won over without words by the behavior of their wives, when they see the purity and reverence of your lives."

Girl, that can't be right! *Right??* God's 2-step plan to help your husband in his obedience only requires that you:

Step 1: Shut your mouth! Quit all the scolding, nagging, lecturing, and comparing. You're the Helpmate, not the Holy Spirit. So, do your job, and let the Holy Spirit do His!

Step 2: Demonstrate your faith! Let your husband *see* God *in* you. The way you treat your husband can help him begin to know that God is real!

And, of course, it is always assumed that a Christian wife is praying for her husband. Prayer is the *most* effective thing you can do to affect your husband's obedience to God, when it's in conjunction with Steps 1 and 2. (And by the way, God expects you to shut your mouth and demonstrate your faith even if your husband *does* believe the Word!)

What can you stop doing or start doing to impact your husband's allegiance to God?

_____

_____

_____

_____

_____

How can I help my husband in his work or ministry?

Are you giving your husband the freedom he needs to do his job/ministry well?

Yes ___ I could do better ___ No ___

Do you let your husband rest and recharge from work without making him feel guilty?

Yes ___ I could do better ___ No ___

Does he know that you value his contribution to his family and household?

Yes ___ I could do better ___ No ___

Psst… Your words hold power! Don't underestimate the impact of an encouraging word to help your husband *feel* great about his contribution, ministry, or what he does for a living.

How can I help my husband love me?

You need to own that question, sister, because your husband may have:

Grown up with a mom who did or didn't do certain things for him, which conditioned him to do or not do certain things for himself or for you.

Grown up with a dad who treated his mom in ways that were good or bad or a little of both, which conditioned him to do or not do certain things to you, with you, and for you.

Grown up with other boys, who picked their noses and thought passing gas was hilarious. They played fake battles with light sabers, video games, watched UFC fights and action movies. They talked smack with each other, which they thought was conversation. Your husband has been conditioned by his guy friends. They influenced what he considers to be a good relationship.

But now he's married to you, and you're not his mom. He's not his dad. And you're nothing like his buddies.

Can you just accept that your husband doesn't have a *clue* how to love YOU unless you help him? And, girl, you're going to have to help him on a daily basis! This isn't one-and-done, "I told you that already" kind of stuff. This is a lifetime of training (Oh, Lord, give us patience!), as you help him learn how to love YOU. But just to keep things fair, you don't know how to automatically love your husband well, either! So, there's learning to be done on both sides!

And if you have daughters, you've got to help your husband with them! The dude barely knows how to navigate you with all that makes you female. For sure, he doesn't know how to navigate all the words, moods, and feelings flowing from his daughters! So, help your husband be *great* in your daughters' eyes!

Sometimes we believe the lie that "if he loved me, he would know me by now." But your husband needs your *help* to love you well! Name one thing you can share with your husband that could help him love you better.

_____

_____

_____

_____

_____

2. The Mom: A Partner with your Husband as a Parent

When God created people, He wanted them to be "fruitful and multiply" (Genesis 1:28). This is a Captain Obvious statement, but men simply can't do that without our help!

So, God has physiologically and emotionally designed us to be moms, even if we haven't conceived a child or we're unable to conceive – *we're still divinely designed to nurture.*

Genesis 3:20 reads, *"Adam named his wife Eve because she would become the mother of all the living."*

That verse is important because we see that a wife can *become* a mother, but our primary role in marriage is to be the wife. *Becoming* a mom doesn't take preeminence over *being* a wife. So, it's *always* wife first, mom second. Read that last sentence again and let it sink in!

In God's design, motherhood isn't supposed to happen *before* becoming a wife, and once we are wives, motherhood doesn't morph into the more important role. I know that's a counter-cultural statement because the world, our family, and all our girlfriends are saying:

Girl, you had better put your children before that man.

Ain't no man deserve to be your #1.

Yes, marriage matters, but those little ones only get one childhood, so they need to be your priority!

Let his mom take care of him; you focus on those who call you mom!

But your help doesn't *partner* with your husband if you put your children *before* him because you're supposed to be a team! Plus, you run the risk of your husband feeling unnecessary in your life or his children's lives.

Putting children before a husband works against a husband's self-esteem (whether he knows it or not) and actually tears down the family dynamic. *It also doesn't do your children any real good.* It generally only helps them become entitled and self-absorbed. They can begin to believe that the whole world revolves around them because their home revolves around them.

Putting your children ahead of your husband is a marital model that is outside of God's design and violates His relational laws. Apart from an intervention from God, your children will go on to repeat the broken model they were raised in, if or when they get married.

Read *Acts 3:19*. God stands ready to forgive. If we're moms, *all* of us have put our children ahead of our husbands in one way or another. Take a moment to write out a prayer of confession and repentance. Today can be a fresh start in your marriage and with your children.

----

3. The Co-Laborer: A Partner in God's Plan

God's idea of a Dream Team is His image, male and female, working together in unity, caring for the earth and its people, starting families, and reflecting the attributes of His divine nature while advancing the culture of the Kingdom of God *together* in all spheres of life. That's seriously beautiful.

Genesis 1:27-28

"God created mankind in His own image, in the image of God He created them; male and female He created them. God blessed them and said to them, 'Be fruitful and increase in number; fill the earth and subdue it. Rule over the fish in the sea and the birds in the sky and over every living creature that moves on the ground.'"

Women are commanded by God to help as co-rulers and co-managers *alongside* men. That's God's plan, both inside and outside the church.

Identify some things you do in collaboration with men on the job, in the church, etc.

Married or Single – Purpose is Purpose!

You want to know something super cool? God created women to contribute as a Helpmate whether they're single or married!

1 Corinthians 7:34-35

"An unmarried woman or virgin is concerned about the Lord's affairs. Her aim is to be devoted to the Lord in both body and spirit. But a married woman is concerned about the affairs of this world – how she can please her husband. I am saying this for your own good, not to restrict you, but that you may live in a right way, in undivided devotion to the Lord."

The Apostle Paul says that a woman's primary devotion is always to God. If she marries, that devotion doesn't go away, it gets divided. Good golly, Miss Molly, that's important to understand! Her devotion is divided because now she must be devoted to both God *and* her husband.

Everything we're called to do *physically* in marriage, we're already called to do *spiritually* in Christ out of our devotion to Him. In the previous section, we saw that God designed our help to function in three distinct ways physically: as the Helpmate, as a Mom, and as a Co-laborer. Those same roles have a spiritual parallel. Let's explore!

The Bride of Christ: The Wife

The Bible literally calls us the Bride of Christ whether we're married or single, male or female. Look up *2 Corinthians 11:2-3*. As the Bride of Christ, how does that image shape your understanding of what wholehearted devotion to God looks like?

_____

_____

_____

Spiritual Mothers for Christ: The Mom

In the Bible, spiritual motherhood has nothing to do with chronological age, marital status, or having had children of your own. Look up *Titus 2:3-5*. How does this passage help you understand your call to spiritually nurture other women?

_____

_____

_____

_____

_____

Fellow workers with Christ: The Co-Laborer

The gifts of the Holy Spirit are given equally whether we're married or single, male or female! We co-labor with Christ alongside men to advance the Gospel and the Kingdom of Heaven on earth. Look up *Romans 12:4-8*. How does this passage help you understand your role as a co-laborer with Christ?

_____

_____

_____

_____

_____

Here's the point, sweet sister: You don't *become* the help when you get married. If you're a woman, you've *been* the help. Marriage just means that your help gets divided between your spiritual family and your physical family, to include your contribution to the world around you.

Let's recap:

> Women are empowered with influence to contribute to *God's* purpose for their husbands.

> It's always wife first, mom second in God's marital plan.

> In God's creation design, men and women do God's work *together* in the family, on the earth, and in the Church.

> Women don't become Helpmates when they marry. Married or single, we are *already* Helpmates by design.

For Pete's Sake, *Help* the Brother

Now let's take a look at one of those crucifying verses that has resurrection life on the other side of it!

Proverbs 12:4

"A wife of noble character is her husband's crown, but a disgraceful wife is like decay in his bones."

In the Hebrew, the word translated "disgraceful" or "shameful" literally means disappointed, to put to shame, to bring confusion, and to become dry.

We all know that "dry" is a euphemism for someone who lacks warmth and enthusiasm or is blunt and disengaged. It implies that someone is critical, bored (or boring!), or both.

Now let's read that verse again with this fuller meaning incorporated into it:

"A wife of noble character is her husband's crown, but a wife who is *disappointed* in her husband, who *puts him to shame*, who *causes confusion* and has become *blunt and disengaged, lacking warmth and enthusiasm,* is like decay in his bones."

Self-reflection is rarely fun, but it's helpful. Take a moment, and just be honest with yourself. Are disappointment, shame, confusion or dryness hindering your relationship with your husband?

_____

_____

_____

_____

_____

Proverbs 12:4 shows us that our help can run in one of two directions: we can either be a man's crown or a cancer. Either of those is a choice. The good news is that we were created by God to be like a crown, so it *is* possible to make the better choice!

So, toward that end, here are some ways to be more like a crown and less like a cancer:

1. Watch your words.

Constant negativity, ongoing criticism, sarcasm, and insults are NOT help! So, don't believe the lie that kicking a man when he's down will help him get back up and thrive!

2. Stop expecting him to NOT need your help.

Remember, God designed your husband with a *need* for your help. He's not an idiot, a child, or lazy because he needs *from you* what God created him to need *from you*, which is help!

3. Remember that your husband is a human being.

Your husband has a soul, mind, heart, and emotions. He was made in the image of God. He has ideas and opinions, wants and desires. He gets frustrated and annoyed, just like you do. He's not a blank slate waiting to be filled up with *your* plans and agenda for his day or life. He's not a machine or robot. And for sure, he's not an animal! He's a person with a heartbeat that needs to be seen as a human, spoken to as a human, and valued as a human. That *has* to be your starting point for relating to him *better*.

4. Respond to his cry for help!

Most men use direct speech when they talk, which means there's generally zero ambiguity as to what they need or want. Our problem as women isn't that we don't *know* what they need. Our problem is we don't *want* to help them.

So, stop right here. You know that your husband has asked for your help with something recently that you have refused to do. What is it?

_____

_____

_____

_____

_____

5. Customize your help to fit your husband's needs.

Every wife's help will look different because every husband is *different,* and his needs are *different.* So, the way you help *your* husband is not defined by the way your friend, your mother, your mother-in-law, or your pastor's wife help *their* husbands.

This diagram illustrates where we get things wrong and how to get things right. The left side of the diagram represents the wrong picture. Unfortunately, this is the one usually touted in the church. It portrays that a wife's purpose is to support her husband through submission. However, the right side of the diagram better represents what we see in the Bible. Our purpose is to help, not submit.

Wrong Model   **God's Model**

A woman's purpose is to submit   A woman's purpose is to help

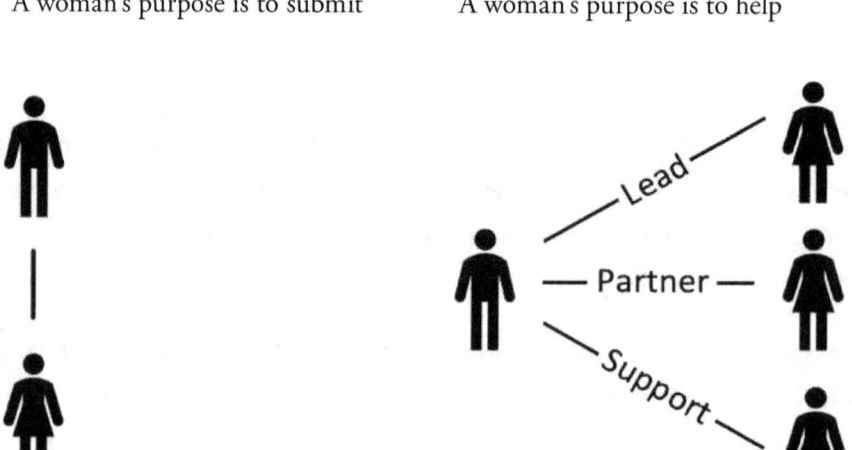

A big mistake with the model on the left is that it equates leadership with headship, when they're not the same thing, and we know it! A person can be the manager of a company without being the CEO or president. So, though headship is leadership, not all leadership is headship. Therefore, by way of example, in God's model, which is based on your divine purpose as the Helpmate:

> If your husband asks you to LEAD the devotions with the kids, but you refuse or resent him for that because he's supposed to be the "spiritual leader" of the family, then you're not helping.

> If your husband wants you to PARTNER with him on something, and you refuse because you think he should be able to do it without you, then you're not helping.

> If your husband needs you to just SUPPORT him, believe in him, or be his cheerleader, and you won't, you're not helping.

Seriously, this isn't rocket science - helping is helping! So, lead, partner, and support your husband the way that's beneficial to him and your relationship, and help him do the things God purposed him to do!

6. You have to know your husband to help him.

Most of us don't know our husbands as well as we think we do. You know why? Because we haven't asked the deeper questions or studied our husband enough to know. So, maybe plan a few date nights and try to get to know your man a bit better. You may even need to reacquaint yourself with him because your husband has grown and changed just like you! *(Psst... you can just ask him for the answers to the following questions.)*

What's your husband's temperament? What are his strengths? His weaknesses?

_____

_____

_____

_____

_____

What's your husband's love language?

_____

_____

_____

_____

_____

What kind of domestic support does he need from you?

_____

_____

_____

_____

What energizes and de-energizes him?

_____

_____

_____

_____

What are his spiritual gifts or God-designed passions?

_____

_____

_____

_____

What is something you do that wears him out or gets on his last nerve?

_____

_____

_____

_____

_____

What's his big adventure? Dream? On his bucket list?

_____

_____

_____

_____

_____

A Man's Perspective by Eli

→ A wife's silence will get a husband's attention better than words. Not everything a wife thinks needs to be said. Also, most things don't need to be constantly repeated. We heard you the first time. Don't dilute your power by repeating your message. We'll pay more attention!

→ A woman's confidence in her husband is the fuel that gets him where he wants to be. If you make your husband feel like Superman – he will do super things in his career, for your marriage, and for you.

→ Berating a man, especially in front of others, including your children, to "spur him into action" is not motivation. It's castration.

Which "Man's Perspective" caught your attention and why?

_____

_____

_____

_____

_____

Words of Declaration

Let these statements become part of your prayer this week. Saying them out loud individually and/or with your group can be powerful. With Jesus's help:

I will surround, protect, aid, and bring relief to my husband.

I will do my part to help my husband fulfill God's plan and will for his life.

I will contribute to both my spiritual family and physical family.

I will take the time, and make the effort, to understand where my husband needs my help.

I will choose to be a crown and not a cancer.

In Jesus's name. Amen.

CHAPTER 5

Submission:
Our Power in Marriage
Part 1

Scripture Memory Verse
"Submit to one another out of reverence for Christ."
Ephesians 5:21

How We *Really* Feel About Submission!

We're in a culture that prizes independence and strives for equality, which makes the idea of a wife submitting to her husband sound ridiculously outdated and, honestly, even troubling. We can't escape the reality that the word submission has been misused for generations to hold women down, hold them back, and hold them hostage to manipulative behavior. Some women grew up seeing their mothers devalued and even endure abuse under the guise of "being submissive."

Sometimes, women resist the idea of submission because they simply misunderstand the concept. Other women recoil at the thought because they haven't recovered from their past wounds or painful experience in the name of submission.

Many of us, whether we're Christian or not, hear the word "submission" and immediately think of oppression and a loss of identity, rights, and control. Seriously, what woman is willingly signing up for that!

So, which is it? Are we voiceless servants, or co-partners, or can we be large and in charge? Well, if we really want to know the answer, we need the Bible. But before we dig in, what's your gut reaction to the idea of submission?

_____

_____

_____

_____

_____

Gaining a Biblical Perspective

We have already learned that women were created to help, not to submit. However, submission is *still* a foundational component in God's design for marriage because it's one of His relational laws based on His own divine nature. As a relational law, submission applies to both men and women. This is why God commands the Body of Christ to submit to one another irrespective of gender (Ephesians 5:21).

God is always the blueprint for our relationships, so we see the precedent for submission in Jesus's relationship to His Father:

"Father, if You are willing, take this cup from Me; yet not My will but Yours be done." Luke 22:42

"By Myself I can do nothing; I judge only as I hear, and My judgment is just, for I seek not to please Myself but Him who sent Me." John 5:30

So, remember those two questions – *Do you believe God is the source of the Bible?* and *Do you believe the Bible is authoritative?* If God is the source, then we'll allow the Bible to renew our minds, instead of trusting our own understanding. If the Bible is authoritative, then we'll allow it to impact our choices. God's Word is not just devotional reading. It's meant to be obeyed and transform the way we live!

If the Bible is meant to be obeyed, then it's super important to understand what the Bible means by the word "submit." However, we really can't begin to explore the biblical meaning of submission until we *first* understand the biblical meaning of "authority." These two words are a package. So, any erroneous ideas we have about authority lead to erroneous ideas about submission.

Understanding Authority

Here is the dictionary's definition of authority:

The right or power to give orders, make decisions, enforce obedience, or to control someone or something

Yikes! That's a popular, secular definition of authority, but it *isn't even close* to the biblical understanding of the word! We discover the Bible's definition of "authority" by examining how it characterizes authority in Scripture.

What do the following passages teach you about biblical authority?

Mark 10:42-45

_____

_____

_____

_____

_____

John 13:3-17

_____

_____

_____

_____

_____

1 Peter 5:1-3

_____

_____

_____

_____

_____

Let's explore what the Bible reveals about the nature of biblical authority:

1. **Biblical authority is the right to rule, not the right to control.**
   God delegates the right to rule based on His own reasons and plan.
   He does not delegate this right based on our socio-economic status,
   education, gender, or any other worldly qualification. Romans 13:1

   *"God blessed them and said to them, "Be fruitful and increase in
   number; fill the earth and subdue it. **Rule** over the fish in the sea and
   the birds in the sky and over every living creature that moves on the
   ground." Genesis 1:28 (emphasis added)*

   *"Then Jesus came to them and said, 'All **authority** in heaven and
   on earth has been given to me. Therefore, go and make disciples of
   all nations, baptizing them in the name of the Father and of the Son
   and of the Holy Spirit, and teaching them to obey everything I have
   commanded you. And surely I am with you always, to the very end of
   the age.'" Matthew 28:18-20 (emphasis added)*

2. **Biblical authority is always beneficial to others no matter the cost.** God is the blueprint for all human authority. God the Father, our Supreme Authority, sent Jesus for our sake at great cost to Himself. Through His sacrifice, Jesus uses His authority to redeem, liberate, and serve. John 3:16; Romans 8:32

   "He forgives all my sins and heals all my diseases. He redeems me from death and crowns me with love and tender mercies. He fills my life with good things. My youth is renewed like the eagle's! The Lord gives righteousness and justice to all who are treated unfairly." Psalm 103:3-6 (New Living Translation)

   "Husbands, love your wives, just as Christ loved the church and gave himself up for her." Ephesians 5:25

3. **Biblical authority protects, provides for, and supports those under its authority.**

   "Whoever dwells in the shelter of the Most High will rest in the shadow of the Almighty. I will say of the Lord, "He is my refuge and my fortress, my God, in whom I trust." Surely, He will save you from the fowler's snare and from the deadly pestilence. He will cover you with His feathers, and under His wings you will find refuge; His faithfulness will be your shield and rampart." Psalm 91:1-4

   "In this same way, husbands ought to love their wives as their own bodies. He who loves his wife loves himself. After all, no one ever hated their own body, but they feed and care for their body, just as Christ does the church." Ephesians 5:28-29

4. **Biblical authority is directional, not dictatorial.** It leads by example and doesn't violate other people's free will.

"The Lord is my shepherd, I lack nothing. He makes me lie down in green pastures, He leads me beside quiet waters, He refreshes my soul. He guides me along the right paths for His name's sake." Psalm 23:1-3

Then [Jesus] called the crowd to Him along with His disciples and said: "Whoever wants to be My disciple must deny themselves and take up their cross and follow Me." Mark 8:34

5. **Biblical authority is never about domination, abuse, or diminishing others.**

    "Son of man, prophesy against the shepherds of Israel; prophesy and say to them: This is what the Sovereign Lord says: Woe to you shepherds of Israel who only take care of yourselves! Should not shepherds take care of the flock? You eat the curds, clothe yourselves with the wool and slaughter the choice animals, but you do not take care of the flock. You have not strengthened the weak or healed the sick or bound up the injured. You have not brought back the strays or searched for the lost. You have ruled them harshly and brutally." Ezekiel 34:2-4

    "Then Jesus said to the crowds and to His disciples: The teachers of the law and the Pharisees sit in Moses's seat. So you must be careful to do everything they tell you. But do not do what they do, for they do not practice what they preach. They tie up heavy, cumbersome loads and put them on other people's shoulders, but they themselves are not willing to lift a finger to move them." Matthew 23:1-4

6. **Biblical authority is delegated by God and is accountable to God.** People will be judged, punished, or rewarded based on how they handle this tremendous responsibility.

    "Now it is required that those who have been given a trust must prove faithful. I care very little if I am judged by you or by any human court; indeed, I do not even judge myself. My conscience is clear, but that does

not make me innocent. It is the Lord who judges me." 1 Corinthians 4:2-4

"Obey your spiritual leaders and do what they say. Their work is to watch over your souls, and they are accountable to God. Give them reason to do this with joy and not with sorrow. That would certainly not be for your benefit." Hebrews 13:17 (New Living Translation)

We need to understand *these* characteristics of biblical authority deep down in our bones. This knowledge can help heal us and keep us from pushing back against the goodness of God's authority or even the legitimate authority of others.

Which of these statements impacts you the most?

1. Biblical authority is the right to rule, not the right to control.

2. Biblical authority is always beneficial to others no matter the cost.

3. Biblical authority protects, provides for, and supports those under its authority.

4. Biblical authority is directional, not dictatorial.

5. Biblical authority is never about domination, abuse, or diminishing others.

6. Biblical authority is delegated by God and is accountable to God.

Write down the name of someone you know who exemplifies good, biblical authority. What did he/she do or not do?

_____

_____

_____

_____

_____

Write down the name of someone you know who exemplifies the dictionary's definition of authority. What did he/she do or not do?

_____

_____

_____

_____

_____

If you've been hurt by someone's misuse of their authority, forgiveness can free you. Consider writing out a prayer, forgiving the offender.

_____

_____

_____

_____

_____

If you've ever misused your authority (e.g., as a parent, on the job, etc.), forgiveness can free you. Consider writing out a prayer of repentance.

_____

_____

_____

_____

_____

Key Operating Principles for Submission

There are at least two operating principles that are foundational to the biblical concept of "submission." Submission is one of God's relational laws that _allows our relationships to flourish and for us to exist in harmony with each other – if the laws are not violated or ignored._ Let's explore.

First Operating Principle of Submission: The Naming Rule

The Naming Rule is deep, yet simple – the one who names someone or something has natural authority *over* and responsibility *for* what is named. Anyone with God-delegated authority has the right to name, which then comes with responsibility for what is named. For example, parents have the right to name their children and have responsibility for their children.

Now this is where things get really cool. God created the universe and named the Heavens and the stars within it, which means God has natural authority *over* and responsibility *for* the universe (and everything in it!).

God created the earth and named it, which means God has natural authority *over* and responsibility *for* the earth.

God created Adam and named him, which means God had natural authority and responsibility *for* Adam.

Then God created the animals but told *Adam* to name them. In that moment, God gave Adam delegated authority to name the animals God created. That meant, Adam had natural authority *over* and responsibility *for* the animals! And that was important because God told Adam to manage the Garden and the earth, which would be hard to do if he didn't have authority over the animals on the earth.

It gets even cooler. The Bible tells us in Genesis 2:21-23, *"Then the Lord God made a woman from the rib He had taken out of the man, and He brought her to the man. The man said, "This is now bone of my bones and flesh of my flesh; she shall be called 'woman,' for she was taken out of man."*

God created Eve, but God did *not* name Eve. The Bible clearly states that God brought the woman to Adam and intentionally had *Adam* name her! According to the Naming Rule, that meant Adam had natural authority *over* and responsibility *for* Eve. Wow, wow, wow!

We even see the Naming Rule in play at the incarnation of Jesus. God the Father let Mary and Joseph know that they were going to be the earthly parents of the Son of the Most High God. However, God did not give Mary and Joseph the right to name Jesus because that would have given them authority over and responsibility for Jesus. The Father Himself named Jesus and maintained His authority over and responsibility for His Son.

Now this is *really* important: the Naming Rule has *nothing* to do with someone being better than or less than someone else. It's not about inequality. *None of that* is in the biblical construct of authority and submission.

Jesus and the Father are equally God. Jesus has authority as God. However, Jesus *chooses* to function within His Father's authority.

Adam and Eve are equal image-bearers. Eve has authority as a co-ruler. However, God designed Eve to *choose* to function within Adam's authority, which was *under* God's authority.

So, here are a few truths that form the framework for the biblical authority/ submission paradigm:

Men are not preferred or privileged over women. They simply have a different type of delegated authority.

Men and women aren't competing forces. God has designed positional order to keep us from becoming a two-headed dragon that burns itself up!

Men and woman were created to be partners in marriage, family, church, and work. A man's authority doesn't cancel out his God-ordained partnership with women.

Men and women were designed to co-rule using their God-given authority and influence. When both do that, everyone benefits.

How does the Naming Rule affirm or challenge your understanding of authority and submission?

_____

_____

_____

_____

_____

Second Operating Principle of Submission: The Effect of the Curse

There are four words that summarize all of Christian theology: Creation, Fall, Redemption, and Restoration.

> Creation was God's original plan. Everything was in perfect harmony with God and each other, including people. *Genesis 1-2*

> The Fall was the loss of God's original plan. Nothing, outside of God Himself, was in perfect harmony with *anything* due to human rebellion. The Curse was the result of that loss. *Genesis 3-11*

> Redemption is the re-creation of God's original plan through the birth, life, death, resurrection, and ascension of Jesus Christ, *and* the indwelling of the Holy Spirit. Jesus is saving everything that was lost in the Fall. *Everything* includes our relationship with God, along with saving you, me, what's broken between men and women, sexuality, masculinity, femininity, our God-ordained identity and purpose, etc. *Genesis 12-Revelation 20*

> Restoration will be the New Creation. God will reinstate His original plan, and everything will be in perfect harmony with God and each other again, including people. *Revelation 21-22*

Thank God, Restoration is coming! In the meantime, we're still dealing with the Curse, which impacts our marriages, and so much more. Let's explore two foundational verses:

To Eve God said, *"I will make your pains in childbearing very severe; with painful labor you will give birth to children. Your desire will be for your husband, and he will rule over you."* Genesis 3:16

To Adam God said, *"Because you listened to your wife and ate fruit from the tree about which I commanded you, 'You must not eat from it,' cursed is the ground because of you; through painful toil you will eat food from it all the days of your life.* Genesis 3:17

God had already given Adam work to do in the garden before the Fall. So, what did the Curse do? It made his work *painful and hard* because the earth would no longer naturally cooperate.

God had already designed Eve to bear children before the Fall. So, what did the Curse do? It made bearing children *painful and hard*.

Eve was already under Adam's authority before the Fall. So, what did the Curse do? It made being under his authority *painful and hard*. Say whaaat??

God told Adam that he still had work to do, but it was going to be much harder because the earth wasn't going to naturally cooperate. God told Eve, she was still a wife, under delegated authority, but that was going to be much harder because she would no longer naturally cooperate. Why? Because *she would now desire her husband's delegated position in the marriage.*

The curse did not change our position in marriage. It changed our disposition. Adam had it all, but he blew it in a moment of disobedience. Now everything under his authority resists him – the earth, the animals, and his woman.

Explain the effect of the Curse in your own words.

_____

_____

_____

_____

_____

How has the Curse affected your disposition in your marriage?

_____

_____

_____

_____

_____

Defining Biblical Submission

Okay, now here's where the rubber meets the road. There's what the Bible says about submission, what our culture says, and what our ego says. So, put on your big girl pants and let's get into this…

Most of us, even if we've not had painful experiences with submission, have a negative reaction to the concept because we maintain non-biblical ideas about the word, whether we know it or not. This is because our culture defines submission in a non-biblical way, and we're generally conditioned by its definition.

Here are a couple words that are related to the culture's view of submission that are *not* synonymous with the biblical definition:

Subjugation: the act of bringing someone under control. Domination. Enslavement. Loss of freedom. Conquest. Defeat.

Subordination: to place someone in a position of less power or authority; to put under the control of another, to be inferior.

Some other words that are *not* synonyms for biblical submission are passivity, capitulation, and servitude. These are *cultural* synonyms, which are 180 degrees from the biblical definition of submission!

So, how does the Bible define submission? I'm so glad you asked! For starters, the Greek word the Bible uses for "submit" means: *to subject oneself; to place oneself under authority; to defer or yield.*

Synonyms based on the biblical definition are words such as, *cooperation, respect, honor,* and *deference.*

However, the biblical concept of submission is much bigger than a definition. We discover the Bible's definition of "submission" by examining how it characterizes submission in Scripture.

Biblical submission is *choice*.

You choose to submit to someone. *You* choose to function within someone else's authority. *You* choose to yield or defer. No one forces you.

In the eyes of God, when *you* chose to marry your husband, *you* were also choosing to operate within that man's God-given authority. Yep. Similar to how Jesus chooses to operate within the Father's authority.

And I know what you're thinking because I thought it too! *Girl, ain't nobody told me that! I had no idea that's what I was doing when I said, "I do!"* But marriage was God's idea. It functions under His relational laws. I don't know what else to tell you, girl!

Biblical submission is *power*.

Remember in the previous session when we spoke of help and its power to influence? Pay attention now because this is game-changing, relationship-altering stuff. Submission keeps our help from becoming self-serving. *It's a counter-balancing power that regulates our influence.*

So, God has designed women with two powers. We have the intrinsic power of influence, and the freewill power of choice, aka submission. Both need each other and are actually synergistic. They supersize each other! So much so that we can create a formula:

Our Help + Our Submission = Our Superpower!

When we lose that formula, we lose *all* of our power.

Another way to understand this is to think of your help as a car, and your submission as the gas. Without your submission (the gas), your help (the car) goes nowhere. Why? Because your ability to effectively help your husband is only as good as your submission.

Without submission regulating your help, your husband will stop *trusting* your help, seeing it instead as a form of manipulation. So, if he feels like you're always using your help/influence to get him to do something *your* way, spend only the money *you* want to spend, care only about the things *you* care about, and sign off on all *your* ideas, then he'll stop asking for your help.

Not only that, he will very likely begin to ignore or resist your help altogether. And once that happens, you are now powerless to partner with God to actually help/influence your husband succeed in his God-ordained purpose (remember those three things – obey God, work, love *you?*).

So, throw the brother a bone every now and again, and just do things his way to keep your help honest!

Biblical submission is *trust* in God.

Sometimes, we struggle to submit to our husbands (or anyone in authority, for that matter) because we just don't trust their decisions. Do I really need to tell you that at some point your husband is going to do something really stupid in your opinion? When that happens, you have to *trust* God to deal with your husband *His* way.

Trusting God doesn't mean you can't use your words (calmly!) and make your case as you appeal to your husband's reason. But trusting God does mean praying for your husband and living like you believe that God has your back. Trusting is choosing to let God deal with your husband, whether he's a believer or not. But you need to get out of God's way.

I read somewhere that submission is God's way of getting you to duck low enough so He can clock your husband! But if you're standing between God and your husband, you're going to wind up getting smacked upside your head! Girl, if that happens, then *you* made a decision even more stupid than your husband's! So, trust God, and just get out of the way. Seriously.

Biblical submission is *obedience* to God.

Now this ought to *really* encourage you. Absolutely nowhere in the Bible does God command men to *tell* their wives to submit to them. That's right! Do you know why? BECAUSE SUBMISSION IS *YOUR* CHOICE. It's *not* subjugation. It's *not* subordination. It's *not* forced servitude.

God is the one who demands our submission and *directs* it. It is *God* who tells wives to submit to a husband out of respect for God. That means submission isn't even an issue between you and your husband. It's an issue between you and God!

We honestly need to stop fixating on our husband's voice and start listening for God's voice because believe me, God is trying to lead you to obedience to *Him.*

How is biblical submission different than our cultural ideas about submission?

_____

_____

_____

_____

_____

Which of the biblical characteristics of submission (choice/power/trust/obedience) is the most convicting? What is something you could do this week to align your submission with your conviction?

_____

_____

_____

_____

_____

A Man's Perspective by Eli

→ Your submission will not silence your voice; it will amplify it! Even if you don't agree with him, he still needs your support. Also, if your husband made a decision without you that you don't agree with, let him know that you trust that his decision was fair for everyone involved. Knowing that will encourage him to do two things in the future:

1. Come to you more often before making a decision

2. NOT just think about himself when making a family decision

→ Most husbands do not want to be evil dictators. Often, they are just fighting to be heard! A wife's submission can encourage peace. Most men want to be the good guy in their marriages. They really do. Give your husband the reins, and you might just start to see his wisdom and kindness shine through.

→ Even though a husband desires your cooperation, he doesn't actually *expect* you to just go along with everything he decides. Your words and input balance him. If you disagree but express yourself with respect, it can help it feel less personal. Your wisdom will be cherished, your influence over him will expand, and your words will carry more weight. *Shhhh...Don't tell him I told you this!*

Which "Man's Perspective" caught your attention and why?

_____

_____

_____

_____

_____

Words of Declaration

Let these statements become part of your prayer this week. Saying them out loud individually and/or with your group can be powerful. With Jesus's help:

I will operate from a renewed understanding of authority.

I will reject the culture's idea of submission and embrace the biblical truth about submission.

I will do my part to maintain my God-given superpower by letting submission regulate my help.

I will choose to grow my trust *in* God and my obedience *to* God.

In Jesus's name. Amen.

CHAPTER 6

Submission:
Our Power in Marriage
Part 2

Scripture Memory Verse
*"Do nothing out of selfish ambition or vain conceit.
Rather, in humility, value others above yourselves,
not looking to your own interests but each of you
to the interests of the others."*
Philippians 2:3-4

A Quick Review

Last week's chapter was a doozy! Hopefully you're starting to *feel* better about that word submission! Before jumping into today's discussion, let's recap:

> We often think and feel negatively about submission due to unhealthy or damaging experiences, along with the societal and denominational messages we've absorbed.

Authority and submission are a package deal. When authority is misunderstood or poorly experienced, it impacts our attitude and response to submission.

There are two foundational principles that help us understand submission biblically: the Naming Rule and the Effect of the Curse.

Submission is a freewill choice and a power. It is also trust in God and obedience to God.

Submission in marriage is a counterbalancing power that regulates our intrinsic power of influence. It keeps our help/influence honest.

If the role of a wife had an equation, it could be "Help + Submission = Our Superpower".

Submission is one of God's relational laws that *allows our relationships to flourish and for us to exist in harmony with each other – if the laws are not violated or ignored.*

What Submission is NOT

Now we need to get nitty-gritty with some things that submission, seriously, is not. This may challenge some of your beliefs or even your relational style, but the things that challenge us often help us grow. Let's explore.

1. Submission is not agreement.

Submission always involves a sacrifice of your will. If you and your husband agree on something, then there's nothing to submit to because there's no sacrifice. Seriously, when was the last time you and your husband argued about something you agreed on?

The opportunity to submit presents itself when there's a proverbial "fork in the road," a difference of opinions, two potential solutions to a problem

– yours and his – when your wills are *not* aligned. The sacrifice then becomes choosing his will over your own.

And you *know* it's a sacrifice because it feels like you're dying, like you won't be able to survive the aftermath of *his* will over your own. It definitely *is* a sacrifice to vote against yourself, but it also gives you the opportunity to be a wise woman who builds her house (Proverbs 14:1) and to be that crown (Proverbs 12:4). And sometimes when you're willing to make that sacrifice, it creates an opportunity to compromise and find a new road together that both of you can submit to.

2. Submission is not about your self-worth.

Your value as a human being is not lessened because you choose to yield your will to your husband. You don't suddenly become inferior. Lest we forget, Jesus is no less God because He submits to the Father.

In the same way, deferring to others does not dehumanize or debase you. Honoring another person's will above your own is a godly choice that helps *you* conform to the image of God. Please let that sink deep into your theology, and then into your heart.

3. Submission is not the loss of your individuality.

Submission doesn't minimize your personality. It minimizes your selfishness, for cryin' out loud! You don't lose who you are when you choose to submit. You don't get canceled, absorbed, or assimilated by your husband until there is no more you.

Don't forget – God designed you to contribute *beneficially* to your husband's life. You are on the team that is your marriage. *Your* insight, perspective, intuition, vantage point, skill set, intellect, spiritual gifting, and so much more are essential for your team's success.

Jesus does not cease to be Messiah, Lord, Rabbi, or King because He submits to the Father's will. You don't cease being that smart, witty, adventurous, organized, and whatever-else-you-may-be woman because you choose your husband's will over your own.

Practicing godly submission will hurt, sometimes a little, and sometimes a LOT. Why? Because submission is purifying. It refines us, the way fire removes the impurities from gold. So just remember that God's purpose in commanding submission is for the best of you and your personality to shine.

4. Submission is not blind obedience.

We need to internalize this truth: Your husband does not stand in the place of God. Your husband's will does *not* override God's will. The Bible does not command a woman to *tolerate* sin, *participate* in sin, or *violate* her conscience in the name of submitting to her husband. There are bad examples of women who made these kinds of choices in the Bible, but no command to follow their bad example!

Take a moment to write down what the following verses teach:

Acts 24:16

_____

_____

_____

_____

_____

Romans 14:23

_____

_____

_____

_____

_____

James 4:17

There's also a powerful event recorded in the New Testament about a woman named Sapphira. It will be helpful if you pause right now to go read it, especially since it's *that* good and *that* instructive: *Acts 5:1-11.*

Hopefully, you just read that Sapphira knew about the plan Ananias, her husband, contrived to lie about the proceeds from the sale of their property. She knew and was complicit. When the Apostle Peter exposed Ananias's lie, God killed him on the spot. A few hours later, Sapphira walked in. She was given an opportunity to come clean, but she stuck with their story. So, God killed her on the spot, too. Her complicity as an accomplice made her as guilty as the mastermind of the plot.

My point is this – if you willingly do what God calls wrong or evil in the name of "submission," God will hold you accountable. So, we don't end a pregnancy because our husband says so. We don't do threesomes or watch porn or start swinging. We don't lie, cheat, steal, or defraud people. And we also don't accept verbal abuse, emotional abuse, or physical abuse in the name of submission either!

Remember, God is our blueprint. Submission in the Godhead is about *honor* and *respect*. It's *never* about dishonor, dominance, or abuse.

This may be a hard word for some of you, but it must be said: if you accommodate sin, you're not being submissive. You're sinning, and you've made an idol out of your husband, marriage, or both.

Don't follow your husband *away from* God.

Don't fear your husband *more than* God.

Don't say *yes* to your husband and *no* to God.

Say no to sin. Say no to abuse. No matter the cost, do the right thing, knowing that God will have your back, some way, somehow.

Submission is not agreement, about self-worth, loss of individuality, or blind obedience. Which of these do you struggle with the most and why?

_____

_____

_____

_____

_____

How can "voting against yourself" strengthen your marriage?

_____

_____

_____

_____

How can you say "no" to your husband and still respect and honor him?

_____

_____

_____

_____

_____

Things That Make Submission IMPOSSIBLE

There is so much to learn about the biblical concept of submission! We're barely scratching the surface. It's theologically big and personally hard, but certain thoughts and actions can make it nearly impossible.

Submission is one half of your God-given superpower. It's one of God's relational laws, and a vital part of your discipleship that shapes you into His likeness. So, no matter what your head or heart tell you, you _can_ choose to submit, but not without dealing with some of the roadblocks to submission. Let's explore.

1. Believing and rehearsing negative thoughts about our husbands

This roadblock often happens subconsciously. That means, you've got to think about what you're thinking about! If we're honest, some of the songs on the playlist of our minds sound like: "My husband is an idiot. He makes me sick. I hate him. He did that to hurt me, but he's not going to get away with it. I should never have married him," etc.

Think about it. What is that negative thing you say to yourself about your husband, whether you think it once a year or a hundred times a day?

_____

_____

_____

_____

_____

You have to take those thoughts captive. You can't allow them to live rent free in your head or heart. Those negative thoughts are not life-giving. They will not help your relationship with your husband flourish. They only bring destruction to your soul and to the soul of your marriage.

What does *Philippians 4:8* say?

_____

_____

_____

_____

_____

Write down a positive thought about your husband that you can choose to think that can replace a negative thought.

_____

_____

_____

_____

_____

2. Justifying and nursing unforgiveness

Read this passage OUT LOUD, slowly:

"If you love those who love you, what credit is that to you? Even sinners love those who love them. And if you do good to those who are good to you, what credit is that to you? Even sinners do that. And if you lend to those from whom you expect repayment, what credit is that to you? Even sinners lend to sinners, expecting to be repaid in full. But love your enemies, do good to them, and lend to them without expecting to get anything back. Then your reward will be great, and you will be children of the Most High because He is kind to the ungrateful and wicked. Be merciful, just as your Father is merciful." Luke 6:32-36

Just so you know, Jesus said that. Those are strong words, and Jesus knows we need to hear them!

Bottom line: your Christianity is actually worthless if it never rises above what unbelievers can do. You don't need the Holy Spirit to be unforgiving or unmerciful. You don't need the Holy Spirit to hold a grudge, or to hate or to punish. You don't need the Holy Spirit to be vengeful, or to withhold affection. *You can do that all by yourself!* You can do that with your eyes closed. No effort is even required.

However, we *need* the Holy Spirt to do supernatural, hard things like forgiving our husbands when they feel like our enemy. We *need* the Holy Spirit to help us actually let go of an offense, and to have grace and mercy for our husbands' faults and failures. We *need* the Holy Spirit to help us hit the refresh button when our husbands wound our hearts and pride.

I've heard it said that whatever caused the offense was an *event*, but to be offended or to stay offended is a *choice*. You can't control every event, but you can *always* control how you respond to it.

"Our Christianity is worthless if it never rises above what unbelievers can do." What is something you need the Holy Spirit to help you do in your marriage right now?

_____

_____

_____

_____

_____

Write down an "event" (*a look, something said, lack of recognition, etc.*) that turned into an offense.

_____

_____

_____

_____

_____

You need the Holy Spirit to help you act and respond like a believer. What is the Spirit prompting you to do so that you can heal from the event (*forgiveness, personal counseling, marriage counseling, find resources, find a group, etc.*)?

_____

_____

_____

_____

_____

3. Disrespect

This might come as a surprise, but disrespect is not a Fruit of the Spirit, ladies. It is not a godly characteristic. Disrespect is like Kryptonite. You literally weaken your husband's love for you and work against his desire to please you when you disrespect him. Not to mention that disrespect does not edify him or help him conform to God's image!

I know this firsthand because disrespect is a major stumbling block for me. I am always on guard against it, but sometimes I'm found sleeping at my guard post. And don't fool yourself: you can choose to vote against yourself and do something his way while still communicating disrespect before, during, and after.

So, you've got to manage yourself, woman! You've also got to manage those things that legitimately annoy you and work against your ability to respect your husband. Remember, you've got to *help* the brother love you! If he's doing something that eats away at your respect for him, tell him for cryin' out loud. Make sure you communicate in a constructive way. Odds are, he doesn't even know he's that far under your skin!

What is something your husband says or does that breeds disrespect in you? Pray, and then have the conversation without turning it into a big tra-la-la.

_____

_____

_____

_____

_____

You Will Reap What You Sow

We're getting close to the end of our submission talk. I know some of you are saying, "Oh, thank God this is almost over!" We're going to wrap it up with a natural law that has a spiritual counterpart. It's called the Law of the Harvest:

1. You will reap *what* you sow

2. You will reap *later* than when you sow

3. You will reap *more* than what you sow

There's no other way to say this, so I'm just going to say it. If you regularly sow a lack of submission in your marriage, then you're going to reap a negative harvest. However, it will come *later and* be *much more* than you want to reap. Let's explore.

The Negative Harvest in Your Husband

You wind up with a man who is both passive and confused. He hears you say that you want him to lead the family but when he tries, you refuse to follow. After going down this road several times with you, he just gives up trying. But that just makes you angry because he doesn't take charge of anything and you have to do everything by yourself. So, then he tries again to lead, but you won't follow. And it starts all over again. The result? He becomes uninvolved: with you, his kids, the house...and you end up not liking him anymore.

He starts to drift away from you. A man's emotional health and self-esteem are deeply tied to his need for respect and admiration. When a man doesn't regularly receive these from his wife, he's more inclined to gravitate toward whatever or whomever will provide it. So, if everyone thinks your husband is a great, funny, smart, or an inspirational guy, but you think he's an idiot and take no pleasure in him, then he's more apt to drift toward the people and things that make him feel good about himself.

Now don't get me wrong. If he does that, especially if that drift is toward another woman, he is accountable to a just God for his choices. But you're responsible to a just God for your choices, too.

The Negative Harvest in Your Home

Seriously, a two-headed dragon will eventually burn itself up! If you're both trying to be the head, then you're going to sabotage the marriage. You're going to have a home filled with anger and fighting instead of mutual respect, love, and a little friendliness!

The Negative Harvest in You

If *you're* characterized by a lack of submission, you'll experience a loss of intimacy with your husband, and will probably notice a loss of intimacy with God. You'll feel like God is distant, and your husband will feel less like the man you love and more like a really bad roommate.

But you'll also wind up with two versions of yourself: the you that shows up in the privacy of your home and then a very different you that shows up at church or work. That kind of duality works against you, undermining your own self-esteem until you don't even like yourself anymore. Who wants to live like that?

The Blessing of a Positive Harvest

But Hallelujah, *finally,* some good news! If you sow submission into your marriage, the Law of the Harvest works in a positive direction, too! You still reap *what* you sow, you still reap *later,* and you still reap *more,* but it's all good and beneficial things that you reap! For example:

Your home will become more like a haven and less like a warzone.

Your submission will have a positive effect on your children.

A disobedient husband could turn back to God. (Remember 1 Peter 3:1-2?)

You will grow personally and spiritually as you pray for your husband *more* and entrust him to God.

But did you know that biblical submission can help your husband regain his God-given masculinity, too? Many husbands are relationally castrated by their wives, yet deep down, most of us want a "real guy." I know that means different things to different women, but it doesn't change the fact that *you* want whatever *your* version is of a "real guy." Maybe you already have him but can't tell because you've got something of his. Can I say it? You've got his balls, and you need to give them back!

And when you give him back his balls, you're going to see a positive change in your man. Of course, he's got to get over the shock first. But once it sinks in that you're giving them back, and they're his again for keeps, he just might rise up and call you blessed!

Do you see a negative harvest in your marriage? If so, in what way?

_____

_____

_____

_____

_____

Do you see a positive harvest in your marriage? If so, in what way?

_____

_____

_____

_____

_____

A Man's Perspective by Eli

→ When a wife willingly submits to her husband out of love and respect, it awakens something deeply powerful within a man. It fuels his confidence and steadies his soul. It motivates him to be a better leader, provider, lover, father, friend, etc.

→ It's tough being a man these days. Factions of feminism teach that it's not right to be manly. We don't know who to trust with our feelings of inadequacy or self-doubt. Your submission creates a safe space for him to be vulnerably human as a man. He finds strength in your trust.

→ A wife's submission encourages most husbands to strive for their wife's respect. Your cooperation can motivate him to take personal responsibility to strengthen your belief in him and his leadership. He will do much more with your submission than without it. A man wants to live up to the trust you've placed in him.

Which "Man's Perspective" caught your attention and why?

_____

_____

_____

_____

_____

Words of Declaration

Let these statements become part of your prayer this week. Saying them out loud individually and/or with your group can be powerful. With Jesus's help:

I will think about what I think about regarding my husband.

I will cultivate respect for my husband and actively deal with my disrespect.

I will do my part to sow good seed in my marriage.

I will gladly give my husband his balls back!

In Jesus's name. Amen.

CHAPTER 7

Sex:
Our Protection in Marriage
Part 1

Before We Even Get Started

Sooooo, we're getting ready to have a woman-to-woman discussion on sex. That means you've just entered the PG-13 part of our Bible study (maybe even Rated R in your opinion).

I know that some of you are *really* happy to discuss this topic because you've got questions or need a little help or are just downright curious about how we're going to approach the subject of sex.

I also know that there are some of you who are absolutely dreading this conversation, but it's not in your nature to skip a chapter, so here you are: uncomfortable, and probably starting to sweat. But you're here!

Everyone with this book in their hands has different expectations, experiences, and emotions when it comes to the topic of sex. So, it's important that you know what I'm saying and *not* saying because we all know what can happen when we assume! Plus, our assumptions often lead us to mishear, which can lead to faulty conclusions, missed applications, or even getting offended.

Please read each of the following points carefully, as they form the framework for our discussion on sex, even if some of them aren't mentioned repeatedly as we unpack this topic:

Sex is our protection in marriage. However, it's not the **only** protective element. The arsenal of protection also includes prayer, following God's relational laws, cultivating emotional connection, establishing healthy boundaries, just to name a few.

Intimacy in marriage is a house with two sides. One side is emotional, and the other is physical/sexual. The two sides are interrelated and deeply affect each other. However, we're going to mostly focus on physical/sexual intimacy because for many marriages that's the piece that's either missing or really, really broken.

Protecting the intimacy in a marriage is a two-person job. If one or both of you checks out emotionally or is sexually compromised, the marriage is exposed and unprotected. Pure and simple. One person alone cannot do a two-person job.

Having more sex will not heal what's morally broken in your marriage. For example, if your husband watches porn, having more sex with him won't make him stop watching porn. It's an *internal* choice on his part, not an *external* act on your part that changes things. And if you're the one morally broken, getting your husband to have more sex with you isn't going to fix you either.

No one is blaming you for your husband's bad choices. Your husband will answer to God for what he does and doesn't do. Period. You are *not* responsible before God for his sin, but you are responsible before God for *your* own choices. So, be honest with yourself, and take full ownership of your *own* bad choices.

Your marriage will be unmanageable as long as there is an unaddressed addiction. You can read all the books, listen to all the podcasts, go to all the conferences, and do all the counseling you want. But at some point, the addict has to deal with their addiction, whether that addict is your husband or you. The addiction must be acknowledged. The chaos caused by the addiction must be acknowledged. The addict's powerlessness to fix the addiction without help must be acknowledged. Until then, the pain, dysfunction, and chaos are not going to stop, and this Bible study is not going to help you.

There's nothing wrong with you if you are the one with a higher libido. Most of what we're going to talk about is from the perspective that the husband has a higher libido. That tends to be the most common scenario. But you're not abnormal if your sex drive is stronger than your husband's, and a lot of this content can still speak to you, so keep leaning in.

We're going to keep things real. Bad ideas and bad sexual choices are destroying marriages. So, I'm going to be clear, but not graphic, and honest, but not vulgar. Satan and today's culture have waged a sexual war against individuals and families. This Bible study is one way to step into that battle, trusting that it will lead to victories and stronger marriages.

If you're single, this sexual conversation is about preparation, not practice. In God's design for sex, the only people who are supposed to be having sex are married people, and *only* with their spouse. Single people aren't supposed to be having sex – not with themselves or anyone else. God's relational laws apply to sex, and you can't violate God's relational laws without consequences. So, I'm glad you're a part of this discussion because it just might save you a lot of grief in your singleness or in marriage.

Treat what you hear from one another as sacred. We all have real stuff going on. Some of us are experiencing things we've not shared before. If you're reading this in a group, your group should be a safe space for revelation, confession, and prayer. Be real, be honest, don't protect sin, and don't be shocked by it. The goal of your discussion is transformation for both the one who is wounded and the one who has done the wounding.

This Bible study is not a substitute for professional help. Just like you would go to the doctor when something is wrong with you physically, please consider seeing a counselor or getting some other kind of qualified help if something is wrong mentally/emotionally/sexually. God wants your marriage to flourish, so get the help you need.

Which pieces of our framework set your heart at ease?

_____

_____

_____

_____

_____

As we go along, if something rises up in you that makes you want to quit before getting to the end, come back to this question and remind yourself of the piece that stood out to you. And know this – the point of this *whole* Bible study is to encourage you to trust God and His authority over you and your marriage. God's authority frees us, protects us, and leads us to healing. God will also convict and challenge us, but His aim is always transformation, not condemnation. So, are you ready?

The Bible's Sexual Narrative

I believe there's a sexual story God wants to tell us. We can piece it together from the Scriptures along with some things we know about God's design of our bodies. Here's how I think the story could read:

God designed sex to be exclusive. It is to be experienced only within the boundaries of a covenant commitment between a husband and wife. In this relationship of mutual allegiance and fidelity, God gave the couple the gift of sex. He intended a couple to open His gift as often as they wanted for the rest of their married lives, as long as they were physically able. God designed sex to contain a type of pleasure no one else was allowed to experience, making marriage something to be desired. God created the male sexual organ to fit perfectly into a female sexual counterpart. He wanted couples to kiss, hug, touch, play, and laugh together. God intended sex to be enjoyable for both the husband and the wife, so He put all kinds of nerve endings in their private, sexual areas so they'd experience a pleasure that could lead them both to orgasm. Orgasms aren't necessary at all for procreation. They're purely the result of intense sexual pleasure. God even gave women an extra, special little part that's completely useless for conception and childbearing. It's simply a pleasure spot on our bodies, designed by God just for women, so that we too could experience sexual pleasure in an extra special way.

Bottom line: God created marital sex as an integral part of the covenant relationship. God designed the sexual component of marriage to increase intimacy and connection between a husband and wife. It's designed to be personal and exclusive. When we choose *selflessness,* sex is restorative and protective. It's holy, healthy, and good for both the husband and the wife!

Does this narrative conflict with what you've been taught or have believed about sex?

_____

_____

_____

_____

_____

What part of the Bible's Sexual Narrative resonates with you?

_____

_____

_____

_____

Sex in the Bible

Did you know that sex is referenced quite a bit in the Bible? There is even an entire book dedicated to sex called the *Song of Songs* or *Song of Solomon*. It is a giant love poem filled with sexual imagery.

I want you to read some of the passages in this poem and write down what you hear because for some of us, religion has sucked all the romance out of the *Song of Solomon!* But before you do, some translation is necessary. Why? Because Solomon uses some words and phrases in a sexual way that have no sexual meaning for us in the 21st century:

The *body* of the wife is described as choice fruits, lilies, a wall, a palm tree, a vineyard, and a spice-laden mountain

Her *breasts* are referred to as fawns, gazelles, towers, clusters of fruit (don't ask me why!)

The *vaginal area* is called a cistern, well, fountain, garden, bed of spices, a mountain of myrrh and hill of incense (umm, just so you know, the satellite talking to your phone's GPS will probably say 'no suggestions found' because this mountain and hill aren't on any map of Israel!)

Read these passages from the *Song of Songs/Solomon*. Take note of who's talking (the husband or the wife) and write down in your own words what they say to each other:

4:5-7, 9-11, 16

_____

_____

_____

_____

_____

5:1, 13-16

_____

_____

_____

_____

_____

6:2-3

_____

_____

_____

_____

_____

7:6-9

_____

_____

_____

_____

8:10, 14

_____

_____

_____

_____

The entire poem expresses a sexual dynamic that many Christian marriages lack. So, let's explore some things that can cause the breakdown and, more importantly, what you can do to get back to God's sexual narrative for your marriage!

Miscalibrated Intimacy

Remember, we said that intimacy in marriage is a house with two sides: the emotional and the physical/sexual? Well, the two sides must

be calibrated or the house will not be well built, at best. If one side is completely missing or detached, the house is unprotected and will be plagued by innumerable issues. To experience the Bible's sexual narrative, we must build wisely and do whatever it takes to keep the two sides of the house connected and secure!

Calibration, in our context, means adjusting or fine-tuning emotional and physical connection in a marriage to achieve better intimacy, harmony, and fulfillment. Intimacy in marriage requires intentionality. You can never drift *into* intimacy, but you can always drift out of it.

And here's the deal: almost every marriage begins with the emotional and physical intimacy misaligned. Generally speaking, women tilt towards emotional intimacy, which we experience through communication. We think calibrating means having more meaningful conversation. Generally speaking, men tilt towards physical intimacy, which they experience through actually having sex. They think calibrating means having more sex.

So, in our attempt to improve intimacy, we each offer our primary connection language (emotional or physical) as the solution. *But that almost always pushes the relationship more out of balance!*

On top of that, many couples don't actually want to do the work of calibration. Most men don't *naturally* want to spend endless time talking with their wives, listening to the inner musings of their minds in order to calibrate emotional intimacy. By the same token, most women don't *naturally* want to have sex five times a day, even if they really like sex, in order to calibrate sexual intimacy!

So, you know what that means? Calibration is a *choice* – a polar opposite, freewill decision *that goes against your natural tendency.* God designed intimacy to be cultivated through *choice*, not feelings. And that, my dear, is counter cultural.

All of God's relational laws are predicated upon choice. Becoming a wise or foolish Helpmate is a choice. Maintaining or losing our superpower is a choice. Cultivating intimacy or staying misaligned is also a choice.

When both the husband and wife choose to calibrate, meaning you each bring a high level of emotional intimacy and a high level of sexual intimacy into the relationship, a miracle happens. Both the husband and wife experience positive, personal transformation as they make sacrifices that benefit each other.

When you don't calibrate, you're still going to change, but it's not going to be for the better. The husband who doesn't cultivate emotional intimacy with his wife almost always devolves into a hard, angry, disrespectful, selfish man. And the wife who doesn't cultivate sexual intimacy with her husband almost always devolves into a bitter, cold, disrespectful, selfish woman.

This kind of intimacy misalignment locks two people who once loved each other in a vicious cycle of loss and deprivation. You don't get what you want, so you think it's fair to not give him what he wants. He doesn't get what he wants, so he thinks it's fair to not give you what you want. And now your marriage is dominated by selfishness, not intimacy. The good news is that we don't have to live like that. We *can* calibrate!

What is one practical step you could take this week to cultivate emotional and sexual intimacy in your marriage?

_____

_____

_____

_____

Broken Expectations

God wants His sexual narrative to become a reality in our marriages. However, broken expectations can keep that from happening. You know how broken expectations begin, and how they unfold:

You start talking to each other, then you go out, then comes full-on dating. He's easy on the eyes and you like the way you feel around him. You want to be with him all the time, and you *want* him to want you. You want him to touch you, hold you, kiss you. Some of us wanted our man so much that we crossed our own moral boundaries (and God's!) and had sex before marriage.

The whole time, that man thinks he's hit the jackpot. You like him. You want him. You think he's sexy, *and* he thinks you really, really, really like sex. He asks you to marry him, you say yes, and he's full of expectation about what his sex life will be and then POOF. The hot woman who craved his touches and told him he was the best is replaced by some cold chick who is constantly slapping his hands and telling him to "Stop it!"

And the brother is clueless. You were his sexy girlfriend. Now you're his stiff wife. He doesn't know what happened to you and worse, he has no idea how to get the woman he dated back!

All he knows is that the woman he married is gone, and in her place is this generally irritated, non-sexual, uninterested creature who doesn't even like him anymore. And ladies, that's like a bullet through the heart for most men because now he's married – for the rest of his life – to a woman who doesn't even want him sexually.

For some of you, I know, this broken expectation is in reverse. You married the guy who adored you, was so attentive to you, always wanted to be with you, and you were the world to him. Now, he's distracted and disinterested, and you don't know how to capture his attention again.

This leaves you with the same broken expectation of what you thought your emotional and sexual intimacy was going to be.

If you were "hot" and now you're "cold," write a prayer of renewal. Ask Jesus to help you empathize with your husband's broken expectations.

_____

_____

_____

_____

_____

If you are the wife with broken expectations, write a prayer of forgiveness for your husband. Ask Jesus to help you communicate your feelings to him in a loving way.

_____

_____

_____

_____

_____

Choosing Sexlessness

It goes without saying that a sexless marriage misses the Bible's sexual narrative! But that is a reality in a lot of marriages, often through the choices a wife makes. And as women, we have LOADS of reasons for not choosing sex. Listing them all would make this book ten pages longer! Here are just some of the reasons married women say no to sex:

Fatigue. You're just too tired. You'd rather make love to your pillow!

Busyness. Seriously, who has time for sex???

Weight. You don't like the way your body looks, and you figure he doesn't either.

```
```

Health. You physically don't feel good so you're just never in the mood.

Medication. Some meds put a legit damper on what little sex drive you may have.

Mother-mode. It started at pregnancy, continued for nine months, and now your child is ten years old and you're *still* not in lover-mode.

Dysfunction. You have unresolved sexual abuse and/or trauma. It could be molestation, incest, you were trafficked, etc. You trusted someone who hurt you, or you were taught negative things about sex that create confusion or fear in you. Regardless, unresolved pain has taken a sexual toll on your life.

Disconnected. You feel emotionally distant from your husband, which works against wanting to have sex with him.

Fear. You DON'T want to get pregnant now or pregnant again!

Hormones. You're miserable before, during, and after your menstrual period. This leaves a short window where you feel "good" or "normal," and sex is *not* a priority in that window! Or you're in full blown menopause, so you're hot all right, but it's from a hot flash!

Habits. Your bedroom habits are killing your sex life – falling asleep to the TV, kids sleeping in your bed, doing your quiet time at night…in the bed…next to your husband (Good golly, now he's got to compete with God?!)

Pain. You have experienced pain (first time, after childbirth, during hormonal changes, etc.) and it discourages you from wanting to have sex.

Incontinence. It's hard to feel like a goddess of love if you're peeing yourself all the time!

Just so you know, all the reasons on this list are legit. But the question isn't whether or not our reasons for saying no to sex are legitimate. The question is – how do we get back to God's sexual narrative for our marriages, so that sexlessness doesn't become a norm?

So, let's explore what's on God's list of reasons for a married couple to abstain from sex:

1 Corinthians 7:3-5: *The husband should fulfill his marital duty to his wife, and likewise the wife to her husband. The wife does not have authority over her own body but yields it to her husband. In the same way, the husband does not have authority over his own body but yields it to his wife. Don't deprive each other, expect perhaps by mutual consent and for a time, so that you may devote yourselves to prayer. Then come together again so that Satan will not tempt you because of your lack of self-control.*

Wow! The Bible says we have a "duty" to each other. That word "duty" is defined as a *calling* or responsibility. It's what we *owe* each other. Clearly, God doesn't want our marriages to be sexless!

What is God's reason for refraining from sex?

_____

_____

_____

_____

_____

Based on the passage, why is it important for a married couple to have sex (v. 5)?

_____

_____

_____

_____

_____

What do you think the Bible means by: *"The wife does not have authority over her own body but yields it to her husband"*?

_____

_____

_____

_____

_____

It could be said that the Bible cites other reasons for refraining from sex, but don't miss the point! The Bible hardly lists any reasons for not having sex with our husbands! You know what that means? It means that God wants us to have sex! A sexless marriage (*or* an emotionally deprived marriage) is not part of God's design! So, if you're off the Love Train, you've got to get back on and embrace God's *full* sexual narrative for your marriage!

What are your top three reasons for saying "no" to sex with your husband?

_____

_____

_____

_____

_____

Remember that you're the Helpmate. Your husband can't cultivate a healthy sexual and emotional relationship with *you* – without your help! In order to experience God's sexual narrative in your marriage, you must be willing to invest in your *own* physical, emotional, and mental health. Do it for your sake, and *also* for the sake of your marriage. Here are some ways to begin investing in yourself:

Prioritize your health and well-being. Grow emotionally, mentally, and spiritually. Go to church. Join a Bible study. Go to the doctor, take the medication that will help you, see a counselor and process the events in your life. Just get healthy!

Create margin in your daily routine for rest. Take a moment to breathe. Spend time with God in His Word and in prayer. Take a nap. Turn off the screens and go to bed at night. Just rest!

Carve out quality time to cultivate a relationship with your husband. An emotional connection helps most women make the physical connection. Plan the date night (don't wait for him to plan it!), stay in and play a board game together. Get creative! Just cultivate the relationship!

Commit to self-care that helps you feel good about yourself. Join a gym, color your hair, get your nails done, laser off your chin hairs, take up painting or crocheting or gardening. Just don't lose what makes you feel good about *you!*

How will you invest in *yourself* THIS week?

_____

_____

_____

_____

_____

A Man's Perspective by Eli

→ Intimacy includes hard personal conversations where secrets are shared, fears are expressed, shameful acts confessed, and things we regret doing can be unburdened. If you take the pain or shame of what is shared in vulnerable moments and throw it in his face in the heat of an argument, his trust in you will be buried beneath an ocean of hurt. He may never be truly intimate with you again.

→ You may feel self-conscious about your body, but your husband desires it. Here's a pro tip: don't tell him the stuff you don't like about your body. He may *never* have thought about it until you brought it up! *His* body only knows that you've got a slice of heaven that's just for him, so keep him thinking that way.

→ When it comes to sex, tell him two things:

1. What you like and why

2. That he's done a good job

Which "Man's Perspective" caught your attention and why?

_____

_____

_____

_____

_____

Words of Declaration

Let these statements become part of your prayer this week. Saying them out loud individually and/or with your group can be powerful. With Jesus's help:

I will pursue God's sexual narrative for my marriage.

I will do my part to calibrate emotional and sexual intimacy in my marriage.

I will choose to take care of myself *for* myself, and for the sake of my marriage.

In Jesus's name. Amen.

CHAPTER 8

Sex:
Our Protection in Marriage
Part 2

A Quick Review

We covered a lot of ground in the last chapter, so let's recap:

Like everything else God Created, sex is governed by God's relational laws.

Scripture reveals a healthy perspective on sex, showing that God intended marital intimacy to be both good and enriching for married couples.

Intimacy in marriage requires intentionality.

Many factors can disrupt or even damage our intimacy, leading to a sexless and emotionally disconnected marriage. We covered three of those factors – miscalibrated intimacy, broken expectations, and choosing sexlessness.

Women can generate a long list of reasons for not having sex. God provides one reason in the New Testament – prayer. *1 Corinthians 7:3-5*

This week we're going to get more nitty gritty for reasons that will become readily apparent.

We already know that sex is one side of the intimacy house, which means it's a priority, just like the other side of the house, which is emotional intimacy. If sex is a priority, then we can't treat it as non-essential.

I've said it before and will say it again – sex is governed by God's relational laws, which, when followed, produce holiness, selflessness, righteousness, kindness, and more. If we let sex become immoral or dysfunctional, we violate those laws. And remember, *we can't violate God's relational laws without consequences.*

Let's look at six things that make sex in marriage immoral or dysfunctional. These are not the *only* things. They're just the six things we're covering in this chapter. Let's explore.

When Sex Goes Bad in Marriage

1. Rejection makes sex dysfunctional.

Generally speaking, God created women with a great propensity to feel loved through emotional intimacy – not only loved, but fulfilled, valued, nurtured, wanted, respected, and validated. In the same way, men were generally created with a great propensity to feel all those *same things* through physical intimacy.

However, the truth is that women can experience emotional fulfillment *without* their husbands – and without ever sinning. Women have lots of options that can fill our emotional cup without compromising our walk with God.

We can feel emotionally fulfilled:

Spending quality time with our children, grandchildren, girlfriends, and others we love

Walking down memory lane with a favorite family member

Going to the beach or on a hike

Attending the concert of a favorite band or artist

Listening to a chill playlist

Experiencing a powerful worship service at church

Participating in a great Bible study group

Sensing God's presence through a quiet time of prayer and the Word

Creative journaling or writing poetry or scrapbooking...

Lying in bed binge-watching a favorite show with a beloved pet

Taking a bath full of bubbles, surrounded by candles, with soft music playing

Reading a book in our favorite yoga pants with our favorite coffee in our favorite mug

Shopping and finding that amazing outfit at an amazing price that makes you look amazing

Plunging into a new DIY project or learning a new craft

And of course we can have deep, emotional needs met by eating a piece of cake or chocolate, very, very slowly...inhaling desire... exhaling pleasure!

So, *even if* your husband doesn't spend any time with you or he has no meaningful conversations with you, or even flat-out rejects you – we have other people, other places, and other ways to derive emotional fulfillment without ever dishonoring God.

Not so for our husbands. God hardwired a man to feel loved, fulfilled, valued, nurtured, wanted, respected, and validated through a sexual relationship *with his wife*. So, when you reject your husband sexually, he has zero legitimate options for sexual fulfillment.

God designed a man to get a testosterone rush every 72 hours on average. It's part of his biology. He can't *stop* the testosterone rushes. Did you catch that? These rushes give him an urge for sexual pleasure and relief. This is God's design to keep intimacy going but you have to participate! Why? *Because you are your husband's only God-ordained, legitimate source for sexual pleasure!*

Your body is the *only* body God has entrusted to him for sexual intimacy.

If he touches another woman's rear end, he displeases God.

If he touches another woman's breasts, he displeases God.

If he kisses another woman's mouth, he displeases God.

If he looks at another woman's naked body, he displeases God. (I'm not talking medical exams here!)

So, what every wife must realize is that sexually rejecting her husband on a regular basis is a great selfishness. I'm not talking about exceptions to sex. I'm talking about prolonged sexlessness that drains a husband's hope and provides no indication of when or *if* he'll ever have sex with you.

If a husband chooses any other way to find sexual fulfillment, *it brings him into direct disobedience with God.* Adultery, pornography, masturbation, strip clubs, prostitutes, chat rooms, Only Fans, sexting, and more are ALL illegitimate options in the eyes of God, no matter what the culture says, or his friends say.

You have many good options to fill your emotional cup if your husband does not. Your husband's only option, if he wants to be obedient to God, is to sexually starve, until you choose him sexually. So, find a way to love your husband the way God designed him to be loved by you, which includes a sexual and emotional connection.

IMPORTANT: You do not *make* your husband choose an illegitimate option. That is your husband's choice, and he is accountable to God for his choices. But remember, you are accountable to God for your choices, too.

Read *Proverbs 5:15-19*. What is God's command to husbands? What is the implied command to wives?

_____

_____

_____

_____

_____

2. Your illegitimate options make sex dysfunctional.

Do you realize that each of us is just one step away from doing stupid? And you might be closer to doing stupid than you think, depending on how broken or dry your marriage is or how neglected, angry, frustrated, or lonely you are.

And just in case you're unsure of what "doing stupid" would involve, it's things like: physical affairs, emotional affairs, online affairs, texting affairs, reading and watching mommy porn or hardcore porn, fantasizing over the guy who smiled at you at the grocery store and said you smelled good, daydreaming about being divorced, longing to be widowed – you get it. All of these and more are unhealthy and illegitimate options for any woman who desires to be obedient to God in her thoughts and/or actions.

When you're doing something foolish, the lie in your mind convinces you that you're truly coming alive. Lies always mask what's wrong as if it's good. So, remember – you reap what you sow, *later*, and more than you sowed. Whatever the temptation is or whoever he (or she) is, it's not worth the damage to your soul, marriage, and relationship with God!

What is the warning in these verses:

Proverbs 14:12

_____

_____

_____

_____

_____

Jeremiah 17:9-10

_____

_____

_____

_____

_____

Galatians 6:7-8

_____

_____

_____

_____

_____

3. Pornography makes sex dysfunctional.

If your husband needs to view porn in order to have sex with you, then you've become a commodity. That's why you probably feel used, lonely, or hollow because deep down you know it's not *you* he's excited about. He's aroused because he's watching other people have sex. He's not necessarily excited that he's having sex with you.

And if *you* need to read *that* book or watch porn in order to get into the mood, that's like believing that you can't enjoy a steak dinner unless it's been seasoned with arsenic! Porn is poison, ladies. You get some sex, but you also kill off the emotional intimacy you were meant to experience with your husband.

Porn corrupts sex. It does *not* make it more intimate.

Porn perverts sex.

Porn is 100% flesh and 0% intimacy.

Porn trains your brain to crave lust, not love.

Porn rewires your spirit to reject a holy covenant and chase an unholy counterfeit.

Porn slowly kills your capacity for real sexual passion and real sexual pleasure.

Porn numbs your soul and dehumanizes you and others.

God created sex to be private and exclusive. Porn introduces strangers into your marriage bed. Do everything in your power to get your sex life back to God's sexual narrative!

What do these verses teach about lust:

Matthew 5:27-30

_____

_____

_____

_____

_____

Hebrews 13:4

_____

_____

_____

_____

_____

4. Masturbation makes sex dysfunctional.

Masturbation is fake sex. Pure and simple. It's rooted in selfishness with no intimacy required whatsoever. Together with emotional intimacy, God designed marital sex to keep two people constantly connected with each other. Masturbation circumvents the Creator's design! Habitual masturbation also has negative repercussions in marriage:

You don't need each other sexually anymore. Your husband is masturbating in front of his screen, using his own hand while watching images you can't compete with. And you're relieved that he's "done the deed" for you, so you don't have to be bothered. And if you're doing the same thing, you don't need your husband either.

You can't satisfy each other anymore. When your husband has conditioned himself to respond to the pressure and friction *of his own hand,* your "cistern" or "garden" eventually won't satisfy him. Why? Because you can't create the kind of pressure he can create with his hand! Similarly, if you condition yourself by your own hand or vibrator, eventually, your husband's approach and sometimes even his natural equipment won't be able to do much for you either.

It doesn't matter what anyone says or what you've conditioned yourself to believe. Masturbation is anti-intimacy. It's self-directed, self-oriented, self-service sex, which is the polar opposite of God's design for marital sex!

What do these verses teach about your body:

1 Corinthians 6:18-19

_____

_____

_____

_____

_____

1 Thessalonians 4:3-5

_____

_____

_____

_____

_____

5. Sexual Addiction makes sex dysfunctional.

Generally speaking, sexual addiction rarely starts after the marriage begins. If you married an addict:

Some of you knew about the addiction but didn't think it was a big deal. Now it is.

Some of you knew about the addiction but thought you could save him from it. But you can't.

Some of you *didn't* know about the addiction until he confessed. You feel betrayed and devastated.

Some of you *didn't* know about the addiction until you caught him in it. You feel betrayed, devastated, and you don't know how to unsee it.

And if *you* are the one sexually addicted, don't try to justify your addiction. You need to get help and stop what you're doing.

Every addict needs to do the hard work of healing and rebuilding trust. Every person who's been betrayed needs to do the hard work of grieving and forgiving. The good news is that *both* the betrayer and the betrayed can heal. God has made it possible for our souls, minds, and emotions to heal, just like He made it possible for our bodies to heal.

The sad truth is that there's no guarantee that a marriage will survive addiction. However, there is a guarantee that you can be made whole, if you keep walking with Jesus through the healing process.

What do these verses teach about addiction:

John 8:34

_____

_____

_____

_____

_____

Romans 6:16-18

_____

_____

_____

_____

_____

6. When he doesn't choose you, it makes sex dysfunctional.

There are several reasons why a man might stop pursuing his wife sexually:

Sometimes it's physical. His body is not cooperating due to age, low testosterone levels, health issues, or the medication he's taking. He could be experiencing stress or fatigue, and so he just doesn't have it in him. He would pursue you if he could, but he can't, so he doesn't. You need to be a wise woman and find ways to encourage him. Help him get to the doctor if necessary. You also need to be patient and cultivate the emotional side of intimacy – talk with him, work it out with him, have some fun together, and figure out what you *can* do together physically, if possible.

Sometimes it's emotional. Maybe he doesn't want to fail you in bed, or fears what you might say to him, *or worse,* say about him to others. Maybe he's stopped pursuing you because he's angry and hasn't forgiven you for something you said or did (or didn't do). Sometimes a wound or trauma from the past surfaces that he needs to process. Be kind. Be humble. Walk with him as his Helpmate.

Sometimes it's his temperament. Maybe your husband is just that kind of guy who needs to be in the right mood or headspace to have sex. Maybe he needs the house to be a certain way or to have a certain routine in place. So, keep things emotionally healthy between the two of you, communicate your needs and encourage him to communicate his, and create a plan together that meets the emotional and sexual needs for both of you.

Sometimes you're controlling the sex. You want him to want you, but only when you want him to want you. The problem is, he never knows when that is. Whenever he pursues you outside of your invisible window of opportunity, he gets rejected. So, he stops pursuing you, and then you tell him you need him to pursue you. So, he pursues you and you reject him. At some point, he gets tired of the game. He's done with being the bad guy, always having bad timing, or feeling like he's begging you for sex.

Sometimes you're no longer the queen of his heart. He has focused his attention elsewhere. Sometimes it's his job or hobby or a set of friends. Sometimes it's an addiction or an affair. But you know that he's not pursuing you the way he once did.

This often sets something off in us because God designed women to want to be chosen. When we know we aren't the queen of our husband's heart, it generally heightens our sex drive. Everything in us tries to recapture his attention. However, once our husbands start pursuing us again sexually (and we believe our husband has been faithful), generally speaking, our sex drive usually lessens in intensity. Why? Because we feel chosen again and all is right in our world.

Have you experienced a season where you didn't feel "chosen" by your husband? Which one of the reasons above best fits your scenario – *physical, emotional, temperament, controlling the sex, no longer the queen?* If none of these are your reason, what led to you feeling unchosen? (e.g., unrealistic expectations, insecurity, codependent tendencies, etc.)

_____

_____

_____

_____

_____

I know that was a lot to cover, but it needed to be covered. Too many of our marriages operate from sexual depravity, emotional deprivation, or both. This contributes to an ongoing cycle of rejection, dissatisfaction, and unmet intimacy needs. Next thing you know, a wife hates her husband for the man he's become, and a husband hates his wife for the woman she's become.

We need to stop the madness! We need to get the help we need, even if it's psychological, medical, or pastoral help. We need to deal with past trauma and unresolved hurt. We need to be aggressive against addiction. We need to identify the lies and replace them with the truth of God's Word. *And* we need to apply the truth that we learn!

Bottom line: Do the work of restoring what's broken in your emotional and sexual relationship. *And* never, ever forget that God created sex and designed it to be healthy and good, and to contribute to the preservation of a marriage. Therefore, God is totally committed to redeeming what's sexually broken in us, and also in our marriages!

Just Do It Already!

You and your husband must actively work together as a team to get what is unhealthy out of your marriage bed. If you just keep calibrating emotional and physical intimacy, you're going to start experiencing the Bible's sexual narrative for marriage!

Now for the fun part! We're going to end with some practical tips on how to promote good sex in your marriage. These aren't the only tips. There might even be better tips (NOT from one of those magazines!), but at least you're getting some tips.

Pray! Listen, I am seriously one of those women who would be absolutely fine having sex once a year on my anniversary, but that's not going to cut it with my husband! So, if you're like me, you're going to have to ask God to help you make the choice to sexually love your husband. Pray for God to redeem your attitude. Ask God to help you value sex as a key component in your marriage. Don't neglect to pray because God wants to answer your prayer!

Find a sexual rhythm. Talk about what you both want or need. Are you once-a-day people? Every three days? Every weekend? Once a month on Saturday? It may feel weird to put sex on a calendar (not the one on the fridge for the kids to see!), but you've got to do what you've got to do to make it happen!

The fruit of finding a sexual rhythm is that you will feel less inconvenienced. But your rhythm is a guide, not a rule and not a taskmaster. You have to still make room in your head for some spontaneity.

Your rhythm will always need to be reevaluated and adjusted for your season of life. So, this isn't a one and done kind of thing. You need to continue talking about your sex life with your husband and keep making the necessary adjustments.

Think happy thoughts about him. For Pete's sake, you've got to know that focusing on what annoys you about him is not an aphrodisiac! Instead, remember why you married him, how he makes you smile, what you find attractive about him, etc. *That's* the kind of thinking that can help you sexually!

Stop helicopter parenting. Giiirrrllll, you need energy for sex! Most husbands would appreciate it greatly if we were awake! But you won't have any energy if you're dancing around your kids all day. Children are a blessing from the Lord, but they are also sexual Kryptonite. Go take a parenting class if you need to, but start figuring out a healthy wife-mom balance.

Initiate every now and again. Believe it or not, most men like to be pursued and chosen, too.

Sometimes, I just tell my husband, "The park will be open for the next twenty minutes, then the gate will close." Sometimes I get even more romantic than that: I walk up to him and ask, "Do you want sex tonight – yes or no?" You know your husband and what kind of invitation he needs to hear. My husband doesn't need much. Yours might need way more. Just invite your husband to bed every now and again.

Be prepared. For cryin' out loud, maintain a state of readiness! If you've found a sexual rhythm, you know when it's time, but you also need to anticipate those spontaneous moments. Keep your legs shaved, your chin hair plucked, and clean up that bikini line! Let him think you're just *made* that way!

Now, if he doesn't care, but you care, don't make "cleaning up" a stall tactic. And you know exactly what I mean! Your husband is in the mood, and you tell him that you just need a minute to "freshen up," secretly hoping that he'll be snoring by the time you're done!

Set the mood YOU need. Honestly, most husbands just need their wives to show up naked. But women generally need more than nakedness. So, play the music *you* like. Light the candle *you* like. Prepare the bed the way *you* like it. You get the point.

Coach him. Help him help you! You're his Helpmate, so tell him what you need (um, it really helps the whole sexual vibe if you don't come across bossy or critical!). The goal is removing *your* obstacles to sexual intimacy with your husband.

Maybe you suggest that he take a shower, brush his teeth because you'd like to kiss a clean mouth, or put on some cologne. Maybe you need him to slow dance with you or cuddle on the coach or bed for a few minutes, letting him know this is the appetizer before the meal.

Sometimes you need to tell your husband *not* to say a word. You and I both know that they will open their mouths, say something ridiculous, and what little mood we have will evaporate!

Give rainchecks, *not rejection.* If you wanted to talk to your husband, but he told you, "I'm really tired and I don't feel like talking right now," you would probably feel hurt. Those words feel personal, even if you knew he was legitimately tired. Wouldn't you rather him say, "Honey,

I'm tired, but I do want to talk. Can I take a power nap and then you can have my undivided attention?" Now it doesn't feel personal.

In the same way, if your husband is asking or giving all the sexual signs, telling him, "No, I'm tired and I don't want to have sex right now," feels like personal rejection, too. Your husband very likely interprets what you said as, "I don't want sex with *you*" or "I don't want *you*." It would be better to tell him, "Hey, I'm super tired, but I love you, so how about a little sumpin' sumpin' in the morning before you go to work?"

It's a big deal for a man to know that you're not rejecting *him*, just the *timing*. That little raincheck (that you make good on!) makes all the difference.

Which one of these nine practical tips can you apply *this week*?

_____

_____

_____

_____

_____

Read *1 Corinthians 13:4-7*. What aspect of godly love can you implement in your marital relationship *this week*?

_____

_____

_____

_____

_____

A Man's Perspective by Eli

→ Porn is a problem. You don't make your husband watch porn. But I need to get really real, right now as a man talking to women. When you shut your husband off from your body, his sexual urge for you has not gone away. Many men turn to self-gratification, which often leads them to the fantasy world of pornography. No matter how good you look, real women can't compete with images of unreal women who seem to enjoy anything and everything being done to them. However, there's more to the porn problem. The mega-billion-dollar porn industry convinces men that the way porn does it is how everyone should be doing it. So, then he tries it with you, and you revolt! He starts to think he's missing out. That's how Satan uses porn to break up marriages. A husband with a porn problem needs to deal with his porn problem. Sex from his wife won't solve his porn problem, but a wife needs to see how denying her husband sex can contribute to the problem.

→ Good sex is good for the man and the marriage. It helps protect him from giving in to temptation. It can't stop him. Only he can do that. But good sex can help him fight. When a man's sexual need goes unmet for long periods, it creates vulnerability in him. Sex initiated by the wife is *good sex* for a man! It lets him know, "You are still mine, baby!" and that you want him.

→ The thing he's asked for, try it! If he's not asking you to do something immoral or that violates your conscience, then let loose, have fun, and try something new with him. If he's not asking for anything new, then you think up something for both of you to try!

→ Even for a man, sex in marriage isn't just about pleasure. It renews and confirms his partnership and connection with you.

Which "Man's Perspective" caught your attention and why?

_____

_____

_____

_____

_____

Wow! We made it through a really big topic! I hope you have gained some insight into yourself and your husband. You and your husband have everything you need to have a great sex life: God's blessing, the Bible's sexual narrative, and God's relational laws, which allow *our sexual relationship to flourish and for us to exist in harmony with each other – if the laws are not violated or ignored.* All you need to do now is work together as a team!

Words of Declaration

Let these statements become part of your prayer this week. Saying them out loud individually and/or with your group can be powerful. With Jesus's help:

I will do my part to keep my sex life good and healthy.

I will remember that I am my husband's ONLY God-ordained, legitimate sexual option.

I will help my husband love me sexually.

I will practice offering rainchecks, not rejection, when necessary.

In Jesus's name. Amen.

CHAPTER 9

What Now?

You did it!

You finished this Bible Study! I wouldn't be surprised if the enemy of our souls and marriages was actively trying to keep you from making it through this content.

Did anything out of the ordinary happen during this journey that almost made you quit?

_____

_____

_____

_____

_____

Yet, you overcame! That's a win, girl!

What are your three biggest takeaways from this Renovated Bible Study?

1. _____

   _____

   _____

_____

_____

2. _____

_____

_____

_____

_____

3. _____

_____

_____

_____

_____

This Bible study is not a secret, and neither are your takeaways! Consider sharing your takeaways with your husband.

Now apply it!

What action steps can you take THIS WEEK to begin applying your takeaways? How would that change your life and marriage? What fruit would you see in your behavior, your emotions, your thought life?

1. _____

_____

_____

_____

2. _____

_____

_____

_____

3. _____

_____

_____

_____

_____

Write out a prayer asking God to help you apply what He has revealed to you through this Bible study.

_____

_____

_____

_____

_____

Now lead it!

We pray that this study has yielded some personal and spiritual revelations. We pray that it has given you practical ways to implement what you learned. We pray that you have experienced a loving and safe community with other women who shared this *Renovated* journey with you.

If you completed this Bible study, you are already equipped to help other married and marriage-minded women! The Bible says, *"As iron sharpens iron, so one person sharpens another"* (Proverbs 27:17). You can be that "iron" for other women and in turn, reap the benefit of their "sharpening" in your life.

Write down the names of some women you could invite if you decided to start a group:

_____

_____

_____

_____

_____

If there are names on that list, God is already at work! Now pray for the courage to invite them and others, then pick a date, and start leading a group. Don't overthink it and don't underestimate what God can do through your "Yes!" Pray. Pray. Then pray some more, and just do it!

Well, sweet sister, our journey has come to an end. What happens next is in your hands.

May God bless you, and may you go bless your husband, bless your marriage, bless your family, bless your church, and bless your world. *Bottom line:* **just go be a blessing to others.**

Why a Relationship with God Matters – and How to Begin

A relationship with God matters because *you* matter to Him – the One who created Heaven, Earth, and *you*. You were made to know God, love Him, walk with Him, talk with Him, live as He lives, and be with Him forever. Your true identity and purpose flow from a relationship with your Creator. You were made in His image, with the ability to live out the culture of Heaven – what the Bible calls the Kingdom of God.

But human rebellion changed everything. Our relationship with God was severed, and the harmony of our relationships with others and with creation was damaged by sin – a condition of the heart that brings brokenness. The Bible refers to this as the Fall of Man.

Now our lives are very different from what God intended because we have been separated from Him, the Life-Giver. **But God still loves us**, even though we don't naturally love Him back. In fact, apart from Him, we don't even really know what love is because God alone defines it.

When humanity fell, everything fractured: our ability to love God, to love each other, and even to love ourselves. Instead of being informed and shaped by Heaven's culture, our lives are molded by the culture of hell – marked by death, dysfunction, selfishness, division, abuse, distrust, prejudice, and every other form of sin and depravity.

In addition to that, Jesus summed up all of God's commands in *one* Great Commandment with three parts *(Matthew 22:36–40):*

Love *God* with all your heart, soul, mind, and strength.

Love your *neighbor.*

Love *yourself.*

But here's the sad truth: every one of us has broken that *one* commandment because no one has *always* loved God completely or *always* loved others completely or *always* loved ourselves the way God intended. So, we're all separated from God due to the Fall, *and* we've all broken the one command God wanted us to follow!

That's why we *all* need saving – every person, in every generation, and in every culture. Humanity has hit an iceberg, and we're all on the Titanic. So, God isn't sending people to hell. For crying out loud, we're already on a sinking ship headed there! **And the Good News is this:** God is rescuing us off the Titanic!

The Rescuer has always been God's Son, Jesus Christ. His coming is our new beginning. Jesus is what Christmas, Good Friday, and Easter are all about. The Old Testament foretold His arrival, the nation of Israel existed to bring Him forth, the Gospels reveal Him, and the rest of the New Testament explains His Kingdom and mission on our behalf.

Through Jesus's life, death, resurrection, *and* ascension, He came to:

Reunite us to the Father *(John 14:6; 1 Peter 3:18)*

Restore God's image in us *(Romans 8:29; 2 Corinthians 3:18)*

Reconcile us to one another *(Hebrews 10:24–25; 1 John 1:3, 5–7)*

Return us to His Kingdom *(Matthew 5:3–8; 6:33; Luke 12:32)*

146

Reestablish our God-ordained purpose *(John 15:8, 16; 2 Corinthians 5:15–21; 1 Peter 2:5, 9)*

Reinstate our co-rule with Him *(Ephesians 2:1–10; Revelation 1:6)*

To return to the Titanic analogy: Jesus not only gets us off a sinking ship – He places us in His boat, called the Kingdom of God. While in that boat, God begins an *internal* and *eternal* work, transforming us through His Spirit. We start to experience His peace, forgiveness, and wholeness, and He calls us to join Him in helping others off the Titanic.

And do you know how it all begins? With three simple, life-giving words that lead to three powerful, life-changing steps:

Believe.

Trust that Jesus is the Son of the Living God. Through Him, God the Father has made your rescue possible. Jesus is the Way to God, the Truth about God, and the Life of God in you. Believe, and then keep believing – grow in your knowledge of God through reading the Bible and let its truth renew your mind. *John 1:12-13, 17:3, 20:31*

Repent.

Turn completely around! Walk away from the world's ways, from your sin, and from ruling your own life, and run to God. Repent, and then keep repenting – release your grip on self-rule every single day. Allow God's loving rule to transform who you are, heal what's broken, and bring wholeness to every area of your life and relationships. *Acts 3:19; Romans 2:4; 1 John 1:9*

Follow Jesus.

Walk with Him. Learn from Him. Imitate Him. Spend time with Jesus, both in His Word and in community with His people, the Church. Let those interactions encourage you and challenge you. Follow, and then keep following Him – learn how to love God and invest meaningfully in the lives of others, even helping some take the same three steps that transformed your life. *Matthew 4:19; Luke 9:23; Ephesians 5:1-2*

And the promise of God is this: if you choose to walk with Jesus now, you will walk with Him forever. Wherever Jesus is, that's where those who love Him will be, too. And your forever with God can start right now with your surrender. *John 12:25-26, 14:3*

A Prayer of Surrender

Lord Jesus, I say YES. You have been waiting for me. Here I am. I give You my body, mind, soul, and heart. I want to live Your dream for me and walk in the wholeness and freedom of a new beginning. Thank You for Your life, death, resurrection, and ascension that make life with You possible. Thank You for Your forgiveness and my restoration. My life is Yours. Fill me with Your Spirit, receive me into Your Kingdom, and teach me how to live and love in a way that gives You pleasure. Change me from the inside out. Amen.

In Their Own Words

Testimonies from Women

Renovated was nothing short of amazing! We saw the Holy Spirit begin to recalibrate and rebuild women's lives and marriages. There were tears of sorrow and surrender, and I have faith that this is only the beginning of what the Lord is going to do! We have tasted and seen and KNOW that the Lord is GOOD. – Alexis

Wow! God was in our midst during the *Renovated* conference, and He is continuing to work in us and our marriages. Most of us are already experiencing deeper connections with our spouses as we started applying what we learned. The content is just powerful! – Peachie

Renovated was AMAZING! We had a Muslim woman in our group, two young women without boyfriends, one engaged young woman, and hundreds of years of marriage represented! Lives were changed. Marriages were changed. God's ways are taught, praised, and celebrated at *Renovated*. – Sheri

Women's ministry leaders showed up for *Renovated* ready and eager to learn. We had a diverse group, including single women, and even one who's been married for 52 years! Many said they came solely in hopes of learning something to take back to their congregations, but they quickly realized that their own marriages needed a tune up! God was definitely

moving as Susie presented the content and through our small groups.
– Kristina

Some of the women who attended my *Renovated* event have been married
40 years. Some were newlyweds, and some weren't married yet, but they
were "marriage-minded." I'm so grateful for Susie's wisdom! – Missy

Renovated was awesome! I walked away with some good nuggets to apply
and share with other women and met some amazing women! *Renovated*
is such a much-needed message about God's design for us as wives. – Ivy

Our church hosted *Renovated* and there were so many amazing ladies
who had so many great takeaways. Y'all are looking at a great group of
Renovated wives and future wives! Susie, thank you for your obedience!
– Lucinda

I went to *Renovated* and I am in awe. It was my first time attending, but it
won't be my last! I brought a friend with me and neither of us knew what
to expect, but this content has so impacted me and changed my view
of what a wife should look like according to the Word of God. Single
women need this. There needs to be a *Renovated* for men. This should be
incorporated in pre-marital counseling! – Maritza

Loved, loved, loved being a part of this *Renovated* conference! Truly life-
changing and humbling! The content is amazing, challenging wives to be
better, do better, and step into all that God has designed marriage to be.
We serve a God of restoration! – Ginnie

As a married woman approaching her 50th wedding anniversary, I wasn't
convinced that *Renovated* would give me any information I could or
would likely use. Almost from the first minute I began to see that I was
glad I came. The material spoke to my disappointments, my purpose, my
power, my submission, and more through amazing large group times and
small breakout groups. The keynote presentations alone were well worth
coming for, but the breakout sessions made it so much more. I certainly

wish I'd had this conference available much earlier in my marriage – but it still wasn't too late. This conference probably should be required the week following the honeymoon and as a refresher course on every anniversary! – Carol

What an amazing experience! The content helped me learn things that are not always taught in church. I'm 20 years old and single and want to prepare as much as I can before saying "I do" because marriage is important to God, so it should be prepared for and invested in. – Martina

I was really hesitant to attend *Renovated* because I have become very defensive over the way our roles as women have been taught and presented to me in the past. I was so thankful for how authentic Susie was throughout the conference as she taught biblical truth instead of what society or "churchianity" teaches us about being a woman. *Renovated* was an amazing experience that I would encourage all women to attend! – Stoya

After 16 years of marriage, I so wish I had attended this conference 16 years ago! So many of the self-induced trials we faced in marriage could have been prevented. Even the regular challenges could have been handled so much better if I had implemented this teaching. *Renovated* gave me one of the best explanations of the biblical role of a wife that I've ever heard! The speaker was engaging and comical but also spoke the truth in power. Mysterious concepts, like submission, were explained with such clarity and empowerment. This conference is truly a gem and beneficial at ALL stages of marriage. – Kristi

Renovated provided me with a perspective on being a Helpmate that I had never considered before. I have always wanted and loved to help others, but for some reason it never occurred to me that I should be trying to help my husband too! It seems so obvious now and it will hopefully be a real game changer in my marriage. – Andrea

Renovated has been such a blessing to me! The principles taught are straight from the Bible, but I have never heard them explained that way. We all come into marriage with our own expectations and mine were unrealistic. Through *Renovated*, I learned God's design for marriage and His expectations, which has given me a much different perspective. I didn't know what to expect from the breakout sessions, but they were the highlight for me. We spent time talking about what we learned in the teaching sessions and prayed for one another, our marriages, and for other people's marriages. We all need to know this! – Leslie

Growing up I never wanted to get married, though I came from a great example of marriage. It just did not seem like it was going to be good for me. Now I always knew I wanted children, but marriage was ehh! But after attending *Renovated* many years ago, I realized it was an honor to be a wife. I have since gotten married and we have started our beautiful family. I can't WAIT to come to *Renovated* again, and I want to know how to get local churches in my area to be a part of this since it's been one of my biggest helps on being a wife! – Meagan

Testimonies from Men

My wife has attended seven *Renovated* conferences. This is my favorite women's conference because she always comes home with great content to share and enthusiasm to strengthen our relationship and grow our marriage. Through *Renovated*, my wife has motivated me to be more confident as the spiritual leader of my home for the good of my family. Thank you *Renovated*! – Nathan

Renovated equals rejuvenated. Renovate yourself and rejuvenate your marriage. Society is so quick to forget our biblical and marital obligations by blaming, shaming, and dismissing our spouses. Through *Renovated*, my wife has abandoned these negative marital emotions and focused her efforts on growing our marriage and creating a true partnership under God's Word. But *Renovated* has also impacted me as a husband. Through my wife's example of a *Renovated* wife – fighting *for* our marriage, praying *over* our marriage, persevering when other wives might have given up, God has allowed us to repair and restore the brokenness in ourselves and our marriage. By her loving me as a 100% man, even when I wasn't, it inspired me to be better, do better, and try harder as a husband. We are no longer resentful towards each other, we are renovated. We are no longer disrespectful towards each other, we are renovated. We are no longer broken like we once were, we are Renovated. We are still far from perfect, but God has used, and continues to use *Renovated*, to nurture, refresh, and heal our marriage time and time again. – Logan

The *Renovated* conference is an oasis for my wife and for women of all ages and from all walks of life and faith backgrounds. The results are just too real to deny in my marriage. The conference boldly teaches on the sanctity, beauty, and power within God's marital design and tackles difficult, and sometimes awkward, topics head-on. Every time my wife attends the *Renovated* conference, she comes home refreshed, refocused, and eager to share the things she learned. This has prompted some good conversation between us – conversation we may have never had. That alone is a huge win in my opinion. But I believe that God has used the content in this conference, that's now in this book, to melt hearts of stone, and stir up new hope for the hopeless, while also challenging those with good marriages to make them even better. – Lynn

About the Author

Susie Walther has devoted her life to discipling and training women to be disciples who can contribute to making disciples in their own spheres of influence. She is the founder of The Well Training Ministry, which began in 2004 and was incorporated in 2008. Her ministry spans 30 years and counting, and includes writing and leading trainings, Bible studies, and conferences. She is also actively engaged in equipping, mentoring, and spiritually coaching Christian women in their ministries. Thousands of women have come through the doors of The Well ministry and have participated in the *Renovated* and *Operation Train Up a Woman* conferences.

Susie is married to Bob Walther, and together they have two adult daughters. She and Bob currently reside in Tampa, FL.

You can learn more about Susie's ministry through her website *thewelltraining.org*. Find The Well Training Ministry on social *@thewelltraining*, and their podcast @thewellwaypodcast. We invite you to follow us, join us, and tell others that a women's training and discipleship ministry exists to support them!

Acknowledgments

My eternal gratitude to God who led me to *Bob Walther,* my husband. We are an effective team, complementing each other, and advancing the things of God together, in our own unique ways. Without my beloved husband, and the difficulty of those early years of marriage, there would be no *Renovated* conference or Bible study. But you were patient, and willing to work it all out with me, as God was working things out in me. For all that and more, I love you.

Thank you to *Emily Henderson, Ivy Reeder,* and *Marisa George* who serve alongside me on the Well Staff. We have weathered so many storms together. You have prayed, planned, believed, and skillfully executed so many conferences and events, and keep the ministry running smoothly. We are a small, but mighty team! My heart warms when I think of all the times you've held my arms up and helped me stay the course against all odds. I'm the most blessed ministry leader *ever* because I have the privilege of serving with you.

Thank you to the *amazing team of women* who have supported The Well ministry year after year. There are simply too many women to mention after almost 20 years of ministry, but you know who you are: the Board, Support Team, Group Leaders, Prayer Leaders, Table Leaders, all the women who come out to pray, who help with set up and breakdown, greet, serve in the store, on check-in teams, and so much more! Where would The Well be without all of you?! Where would *I* be without all of you?!

Thank you to my editor, *Tarah Todd*. I needed someone to help me edit my material for conferences and trainings and got a friend and advisor to boot! I love the way your brain works. I love that you know what I'm trying to say and can get it down on paper so that others will know what I'm trying to say. I love our God-talks, prayer times, laughs, and even the times we duke things out over the content for the sake of clarity. You have been nothing but a blessing to me, and I'm the better for it.

And I can't end without thanking, *Eli Gonzalez*, our publisher. I met Eli at an event having no idea what he did for a living, and how God would use him to make a dream come true. For years, I've wanted to turn the content for the *Renovated* conference into a Bible study, but the task was so personally daunting. Nonetheless, the dream persisted, and God made a way for me to meet Eli, who has been an answer to prayer. This project would not have a bow on top if you did not say "yes, I will help you." I am forever grateful, Eli. I really am.

www.ingramcontent.com/pod-product-compliance
Lightning Source LLC
Chambersburg PA
CBHW071236130626
46556CB00003B/1043